A LASTING LEGACY

A LASTING LEGACY

A Helpful Guide as You Walk the Pathways of Life

ALBERT CHRISTIAN SCHAUER JR.

and

PHYLLIS JANE SCHAUER

iUniverse, Inc.
Bloomington

A LASTING LEGACY
A Helpful Guide as You Walk the Pathways of Life

Scripture taken from the HOLY BIBLE, NEW INTERNATIONAL VERSION®.

iUniverse books may be ordered through booksellers or by contacting:

iUniverse
1663 Liberty Drive
Bloomington, IN 47403
www.iuniverse.com
1-800-Authors (1-800-288-4677)

ISBN: 978-1-4502-9324-2 (sc)
ISBN: 978-1-4502-9326-6 (hc)
ISBN: 978-1-4502-9325-9 (ebk)

Printed in the United States of America

iUniverse rev. date: 05/21/2012

A HELPFUL GUIDE
AS YOU WALK THE PATHWAYS
OF LIFE

A Legacy of Biblically Based Lessons and Truths

---

*A Discourse on Behavior and Acts of Faith
to Make Your Life a Joy to God
and Prosperous for You*

For

Brittany, Natalie, and Ethan Waldron;

Nicholas Oliver; Jonathon and Meredith Schauer;

and

all God's children

From

Albert Christian Schauer Jr. (Opa) and

Phyllis Jane Schauer (Oma)

PREFACE

As the years go swiftly by, we find ourselves spending more and more time in periods of reflection and remembrance. We see our life's undertakings, accomplishments, and shortcomings in a more philosophic light than we did during our earlier years. Our younger years were filled with so much excitement and anticipation. We truly believed we had all the time in the world. Oh, yes, there's plenty of time to get the big things in order. Let's get on with the tasks and pleasures of the moment—the education, the job, the house, the clothes, the vacations, and on and on and on. Then we enter a period in life in which all material pursuits begin to lose meaning or desire. We begin to reflect on those pursuits and conquests that have eternal value, those that have lasting meaning. Such is the foundation for this book's existence and such will be the metamorphic of thought, priorities, and undertakings in your lives.

The idea for this book began to take shape while flying across the Atlantic Ocean. We were returning from one of our more than 150 trips to the United Kingdom and other points in Europe during the 1980s and 1990s, and lastly into the 2000s. It was August 1994, and thoughts turned to the pace of life and where we, as a family, were likely to be in another five, ten, or twenty years. We had persistently strived to lead a life of service to our Lord. The lessons learned along the way were so valuable that we felt a need to codify them in our own words. Yet, those lessons and experiences are not unique to us or to our time. The years were clicking along at an ever more rapid pace. It was imperative that we took the time to gather our thoughts and get ready for the day when we would pass from this life to spend eternity with our precious Lord and Savior. But before that day arrives, would it not be a great idea if we left a legacy of truths about those lessons that had guided us through life and had been the rudder and compass as we experienced challenges, pains, hurts, anxieties, disappointments, and sorrows? Could our experiences be chronicled in such a way as a guiding light to our children, grandchildren, and future generations? Could we in some way help future children (when they reach the age of understanding) to find that uplifting spirit that might be needed at a moment in time and to help carry them through a momentary crisis, a period of tragedy, or a period of outright loneliness?

Like so many parents and grandparents, we see life quickly slip away. A time comes when we spend countless hours reflecting on numerous unfulfilled dreams and aspirations. Even though a life is filled with many bestowed awards and rewards, there is that deep feeling of seeing a life passing by without reaching that unfulfilled dream or special wish. Those who have found the Lord and felt His special abiding love know that many of these temporal world missed dreams are nothing more than empty hopes and useless pursuits. The promise of eternity with God far transcends earthly rewards and gives us the courage and strength to press on for that greater and final reward. This book is meant to help lift you, support you, guide you, and encourage you during those times when trying situations arise as you travel the pathways of life. You need to be armed with a special arsenal of tools that, when fully understood and used, will give you strength, courage, patience, hope, and peace of mind. Believe us: *these values and truths work*. They will lift you up when you are down. They will comfort you when you are oppressed. They will strengthen you when all hope is gone. Live these truths. Follow these guides, and your life will be far richer.

At an early age, the love, support, grace, or fear of the Lord is not central in our lives. Sure, we can be raised in a loving Christian environment and reared in a God-centered home, but to feel the true power of a merciful, all-powerful God—one who cherishes the love and devotion of His created ones—grows as the years go by. We found that the love and drive to do the will of the Lord grew steadily and more progressively as we passed the fifty-year-old mark. We cannot consume enough of the food the Lord has given us in His Word—the Holy Bible.

The Bible needs to be your companion and compass, the instruction book and guide for charting your path through life.

The Proverbs give wisdom and insights that have been learned by the greatest minds known to mankind. The sayings are true; the vignettes of truisms go right to the heart of man's emotions, fears, vices, greed, and yearnings. Yet, the Lord always holds out a promise of hope and an avenue leading to a happy, fulfilled life. Not a life devoid of pain or disappointment, but one promising peace and hope during those periods of pain and disappointment; a life that lifts us to a higher level of joy and satisfaction as we draw closer to our Lord and Creator.

The Psalms give comfort and address virtually every life situation. After all, David knew what it was about, he was likely the most despised, hated, and pursued man on the face of the earth. His enemies railed in rage at the thought of his conquests, and even Saul, King of Israel and David's father-in-law, turned on David. From many of his numerous fits of depression, Saul carried on a lifelong vendetta to get at David, even to the point of death. But David always found hope and solace in the presence of the Lord.

The New Testament itself carries a wealth of answers to life's challenges. The Gospels chronicle the foundation of Christ's ministry and His sacrifice for you and us. Likewise, the letters of Paul are powerful and filled with words of encouragement and hope when faced with desperate, troubling situations. In them, we witness the issues facing the early, struggling church. The problems they faced in day-to-day worship and fellowship are the same issues we face today: in-fighting, greed, twisting the Gospel, struggling church finances, etc.

So let us move to those issues that seem to arise in everybody's life. Yes, indeed, as a Christian, you will experience the challenges and pains just as a non-Christian. But what sets us apart is that God, in His infinite wisdom and love, has assured us as His chosen people that if we put our full faith and trust in Him and if we diligently seek to follow His precepts (commands), then He will be there to give us comfort. He will put a shield around us to protect us from the attacks of Satan, and will bridge us through the turmoil by setting us on solid ground with joy and happiness.

ACKNOWLEDGMENTS

The inspiration for this work must rest first with our precious Lord and Savior, Jesus Christ. The Lord gives all good and perfect gifts and without His sustaining grace and power, we would never have risen to the challenge, let alone devoted the time and energy to compose this exposition. There have been others as well who have aided in this cause and without whose help and encouragement we would have long ago lost the drive and spirit to press forward.

You, our precious grandchildren Brittany, Natalie, and Ethan Waldron have given us the hope and joy to undertake this work. As your father (Todd A. Waldron) and mother (Vicki A. Waldron, nee Schauer) have given us so much joy and love, so too have you in many special ways. We can very clearly remember where we were when each of you was born. Each birth was so very special.

In Brittany's case, we canceled a vacation to Hawaii at the last minute. Cancellation of the trip meant nothing to us, because we were blessed with our first grandchild on the day we were to leave. Added to the blessing, your birth occurred on Oma's forty-ninth birthday. In Natalie's case, it was a most beautiful Palm Sunday in April 1992. Your birth occurred on the same date as Oma's very close friend, Barb Miller. Still today, Oma, Natalie, and Barb celebrate the mutual birth dates by getting together for a lunch. As for Ethan, we were vacationing on Marco Island, Florida. Ron and Nancy Niewoonder were caring for the two girls and Opa's call to Ron from a restaurant on Marco Island gave us the most precious news—we had our third grandchild, a boy.

Our son, Tim Schauer, deserves a very special acknowledgment, as he has been a valued support to us, and has been a most gracious and loving uncle to Todd and Vicki's children. His loving and compassionate spirit is a treasure, and he has been a help to Opa more times than he can imagine. To Tim's children, Nicholas Oliver, and Jonathon and Meredith Schauer, and his blessed wife, Cathy, we extend these lessons in the love and spirit of the Lord. As part of our family, we give you these lessons of life to help you obtain the joys and riches offered to the family of God. As of this writing, Nick will be returning to Kalamazoo after serving two and a half years in the US Air Force and will be pursuing his college education in Kalamazoo. Jonathon attends kindergarten at West Christian Elementary, the successor to the grade school (North Christian Grade School) attended by Opa and Tim and Vicki. Meredith attends pre-school at West Christian Elementary.

We extend special thanks to our parents for their Christ-centered upbringing and nurturing. Oma's parents, Walter and Harmiena (nee Schreuder/Vanderweele) Schiedel, and Opa's parents, Albert and Cornelia (nee VanBoven/Braamse) Schauer, collectively laid the foundation of our faith and love for the Lord. While Opa's father died in a fishing accident three months after Opa was born, we still see him as being a part of God's providence in bringing knowledge of our Lord into our family.

And finally to all those who nurtured us along the way in Sunday school, catechism, Christian school, in the workplace, in Bible studies, in small groups, and at church services in the most out-of-the-way places around the globe (Molokai, Geneva, Switzerland, Singapore, Honolulu, London, Amsterdam, Frankfurt, Los Angeles, Johannesburg, Leeds, UK, Florida, Cleveland, Helsinki, Manaus, Sao Paulo, Rio de Janeiro, Oklahoma City, Taichung, and a host of others), we give our special joy and praise and thanks. Yes, we attended church services in all those places as well as in our own home churches. We extend our utmost joy and praise to all the saints for lifting our spirits and giving us the hope to continue with this blessed journey. We shall rejoice when we shall be reunited with Him and sing with the saints, "We shall behold Him; we shall behold Him, face to face . . ."

We also extend a most loving and gracious thank you to Jerry Whitaker, a dear brother in the Lord, and to Todd Waldron and Phyllis Schauer for their willingness to read the manuscript and provide a wealth of valuable ideas and recommendations. And a very special appreciation to the people at iUniverse for their patience and talented assistance in reviewing, editing and printing this work. Without their help, this work never would have been possible.

A very special added thanks and love to my dear wife Phyllis for allowing Opa the time to collect the thoughts, for offering loving insights, and for remembering lessons long forgotten.

February 28, 2012
Kalamazoo, Michigan, USA

The fear of the Lord

is the beginning of wisdom, and knowledge of the

Holy One is understanding.

Proverbs 9:10

PREAMBLE

"Hear now, O Israel, the decrees and laws I am about to teach you. Follow them so that you may live and may go in and take possession of the land that the Lord, the God of your fathers, is giving you. Do not add to what I command you and do not subtract from it, but keep the commands of the Lord your God that I give you.

"You saw with your own eyes what the Lord did at Baal Peor. The Lord your God destroyed from among you everyone who followed the Baal of Peor, but all of you who held fast to the Lord your God are still alive today.

"See, I have taught you decrees and laws as the Lord my God commanded me, so that you may follow them in the land you are entering to take possession of it. **Observe them carefully, for this will show your wisdom and understanding** to the nations, who will hear about all these decrees and say, 'Surely this great nation is a wise and understanding people. What other nation is so great as to have their gods near them the way the Lord our God is near us whenever we pray to him? And what other nation is so great as to have such righteous decrees and laws as this body of laws I am setting before you today?'"

"Only be careful, and watch yourselves closely so that you do not forget the things your eyes have seen or let them slip from your heart as long as you live. **Teach them to your children and to their children after them . . ."**

Deuteronomy 4:1–9

CHAPTER 1

Faith

. . . Because you have so little faith. I tell you the truth; if you have faith as small as a mustard seed, you can say to this mountain, "Move from here to there" and it will move. Nothing will be impossible for you. (Matthew 17:20–21)

The making of this book had its genesis in a desire to leave a legacy for our children and grandchildren, a legacy founded on taught spiritual values as well as learned lessons. The messages here are really nothing exceptionally special about basic foundational values or behaviors. What might make them special is the uniqueness of the messages and that those messages have come from those whom our children and grandchildren know, and knew, intimately. Their very own Oma and Opa, real people they knew, wrote this. These are lessons experienced and encountered by people just like themselves.

He holds victory in store for the upright, he is a shield to those whose walk is blameless, for he guards the course of the just and protects the way of his faithful ones. (Proverbs 2:7–8)

We start this book with a discussion on faith: our faith, the faith of our parents, the faith of our grandparents and ancestors, and the faith of those gallant leaders found in the history of Israel and dedicated followers of the precepts laid out by our dear God and heavenly Father.

Faith gives us a solid ground to stand on. Faith, embraced by hope, gives us purpose and meaning for our lives. More to the point, we want to

1

talk about the faith we trust you have developed and nurtured, the faith we hope resides in your heart, and the faith you carry with you every day of your lives.

Without faith, we have no foundation on which to stand. Paul says the foundation of a Christ-centered life is faith, hope, and love. So too, we will start our book with these three foundations. Without a strong faith, the rest is meaningless. We live by a faith made available through the workings of the Holy Spirit allowing us to know that God has laid out a promise for us when this mortal life is finished.

Throughout the history of mankind, faith has always been at the foundation of man's existence. We, and all mankind, have this need inbred in us to put our trust in something. Every element of our daily lives is founded on faith. We, for example, put our trust and faith in God as the author and sustainer of all things. God in His majestic love and faithfulness provides for our every need. We know that and we believe. We trust and have faith that God will be there day in and day out to feed us, clothe us, and shelter us.

Yet there are those who put their trust in scientific reasoning and state that unless it can be seen and repeated in an experiment, there is no foundation for believing in something. In their twisted way, those same individuals will emphatically proclaim the *proven* scientific fact of Darwinian evolution. They will state evidence that points to millennia of genetic evolvement eventually leading to human life. Yet when asked to apply their very own strict scientific regimen by insisting on the need to observe the principle of repeatability, they will immediately retaliate by insisting one must have faith. Faith in a God is not acceptable, but faith in a scientific principle must be accepted. Simply put, the belief in Darwinian evolution is nothing more than a groundless faith by those who will readily deny the existence of God and outright refuse to accept any supernatural existence of beings or events.

We have been called not to just put our trust in whatever meets our momentary fancy. We are a cherished creation of an all-loving and omnipotent Creator. Our lives are not operating in a totally free-for-all vacuum. For our Maker and Creator has set Himself in front of us to make sure that our faith is sound and squarely fixed on Him.

A life of sixty, seventy, or eighty years cannot progress without a firmly rooted faith in a whole variety of day-to-day activities. The building we work in evokes our faith in knowing the structure won't explode or collapse. We cross a bridge and have faith that architects have designed the structure so the bridge will not give way. We drive our vehicles on roads trusting that other drivers are careful.

The faith we are talking about is far more substantive than those examples. We're talking about a deep conviction that the impossible is possible, that the unthinkable is achievable, and that the unattainable is reachable. Notice how Paul says it in these excerpts from Hebrews 11 (verses):

> Now <u>faith</u> is being sure of what we hope for and certain of what we do not see. This is what the ancients were commended for. (1–2)

> By <u>faith</u> we understand that the universe was formed at God's command, so that what is seen was not made out of what was visible. (3)

> By <u>faith</u> Abraham, when called to go to a place he would later receive as his inheritance, obeyed and went, even though he did not know where he was going. By faith he made his home in the promised land like a stranger in a foreign country. (8–9)

> By <u>faith</u> Abraham, even though he was past age—and Sarah herself was barren—was enabled to become a father because he considered him faithful who made the promise. (11)

> By <u>faith</u> Abraham, when God tested him, offered Isaac as a sacrifice. He who had received the promises was about to sacrifice his one and only son . . . (17)

This kind of faith is one that transcends all earthly comprehension and asks us to accept that without question those human activities and issues that far transcend our human understanding. Now this is not saying we do not quest to gain greater understanding of God's creation and the magnificent workings of the world and matter. No, not at all. For without that quest for greater understanding and knowledge, we never would have uncovered God's desire to have us discover automobiles or airplanes or advanced medical techniques or a host of other mind-numbing technical advancements. God's world is full of yet to be discovered wonders, and He desires that we continue to uncover those wonders, which manifest the power and glory of His unfathomable creation. There comes a time in everyone's life where we cannot understand how God will accomplish His will in our life, or how we will get out of a particular situation, which seems all but hopeless, or how we will overcome what appears to be a career-ending or life-ending situation. Times like these make us feel as if all hope is gone and all solutions are exhausted. We need to revisit the verses from Hebrews. Building on those passages, the following verses from Psalms say it so well:

> **The Lord is a refuge for the oppressed, a stronghold in times of trouble. Those who know your name will trust in you, for you, Lord, have never forsaken those who seek you. (Psalms 9:9–10)**

> **[M]y God turns my darkness into light. (Psalms 18:28b)**

> **In you our fathers put their trust; they trusted and you delivered them. They cried to you and were saved; in you they trusted and were not disappointed. (Psalms 2:4–5)**

> **It is God who arms me with strength and makes my way perfect. (Psalms 18:32)**

The book of Nahum is one of those Minor Prophets we probably skip too frequently in our Bible reading. Notice how he declares his faith in God so succinctly when he says:

> **The Lord is good, a refuge in times of trouble. He cares for those who trust in Him. (Nahum 1:7)**

Faith will support you and strengthen you. Faith will give you hope when all else seems lost. Faith will brighten your day when your friends seem to abandon you. Faith will stand you strong when all seems to be going wrong. Faith will lift you up when the trials of the world seem to never end. Faith will bear you up when your body seems to be failing, when all hope

4

is lost, and when nothing comes to the forefront to alleviate the anguish or pain. Having been in those situations so many times ourselves, let us put it this way. Stay strong in the Lord. Through faith, He will not fail you.

Oh, how many times we forgot this. We always seemed to try to reach down into our hearts for the answer. Or we tried frantically to analyze a problem and rationalize a solution. We could never seem to get to a complete answer. It seemed we were always running into a roadblock. Yet the faith that God placed in our hearts always came back as a reminder. He is faithful, thus, we should be faithful.

This book is founded on faith. If you lack faith, all the rest will seem meaningless. There are those in this world who will mock and belittle your beliefs. You will be challenged to assert your faith in situations that lack any understanding of faith. You will be called upon to reach into your heart and proclaim the faith that has made you a child of God. You were raised as children of God and the faith. What He has implanted in your hearts can never be lost. It can be forgotten, but never lost. When all else fails, return to your faith. It will hold you strong and give you courage.

[I]f we are faithless, he will remain faithful, for he cannot disown himself. (2 Timothy 2:13)

Your faith will grow as you study His Word. Your faith will grow as you study His creation. Your faith will grow as you meditate in prayer. Your faith will grow as you congregate with believers. And your faith will grow as you share your resources in advancing His kingdom. You can see that a true faith builds as time passes. You will see wondrous things in your life, things that defy imagination. You will experience wonders that cannot be explained by mere human understanding. The glories of God are too magnificent to comprehend and grasp by our mortal and feeble minds. Our understanding is miniscule when compared to the boundless wisdom and ways of God. This you must accept. This you must trust in and plant in your heart.

Then there are those times when you must stand firm in your faith. God has given you considerable understanding and wisdom when proclaiming His ways. Those who proclaim more education or those who proclaim more of life's experiences will challenge your faith. There are those who will assert their authority and insist that their way is the correct way. Because of your beliefs, you may be laughed at or feel humiliated.

You may even be in a position of having to make a career choice because your faith conflicts with the norm of the organization. But through it all, stand firm in your faith and do not fear. For as Isaiah once said:

If you do not stand firm in your faith, you will not stand at all. (Isaiah 7:9b)

Be assured that Oma and Opa were called upon to express their faith and oftentimes during difficult situations. When we were working, there was no end to the number of people with whom we associated who were devoid of the faith, the faith that so richly blessed us. During Opa's college days, he was called to assert in examinations that the world came into existence through chemical means and was not created by God. Incorrect answers abounded in the exam papers when we attested to another means by which the world came into existence, that by the wondrous creative works of our all-powerful and omniscient God. Or in the work environment when the company leader proclaimed there could be no God, for how could a God allow such suffering, pain, and injury in this world. Or later in life where so-called educated scientists proclaimed the sanctity and sound science of Darwinian evolution for the origins of human beings. Space doesn't permit us to go into the fallacy of the evolution myth. There are numerous, wonderful publications by eminent scientists, pastors, and philosophers who expose this myth for what it is.

We talk later about the Bible and its foundational necessity in our lives. This is where it begins. The Bible establishes the very core of the Christian faith and the means to salvation. Through study of the Bible, you will build the nucleus of your faith and the strength you need to sustain and proclaim that faith. It is for this reason that we as grandparents, and those who are your parents, are charged with educating you in that faith. This is the reason you have been nurtured during your youth to understand the essentials of our faith. You are called to stand strong and go forth to proclaim that faith, just as countless millions have done before you. Take this charge seriously. Do not waver. Do not weaken. Do not yield. And do not forget the lessons of your faith. It will carry you through the hard times, and it will prosper you in the good times.

CHAPTER 2

Hope

Against all hope, Abraham in hope believed and so became the father of many nations. (Romans 4:18)

The journey of life fills up with a multitude of opportunities, challenges, and frustrations. The diversions soon overtake us, and we begin to question our purpose or our mission. There are times when all hope is lost and all seems hopeless. We feel helpless and all seems to go wrong. Wonderful expectations are drowned out by hopeless periods of frustration. It seems as if we have no possibility of accomplishing any meaningful objective, let alone our specific objectives. Our faith seems to desert us, and we wonder whether our long-held beliefs are of any value. Rest assured the answer is yes and we will tell you why.

Every biblical character suffered from that same sense of hopelessness and despair. When all seemed to be beyond recovery, hope in the Lord carried the day. The non-Christian does not enjoy that insight. God offers hope to every believer and in that vein gives you and us that inward comfort that springs from hope. Contrasted with the unbeliever, our hope is founded on God's promise of surety and trust. Our God is capable of rectifying any situation or circumstance. When all else fails, our trust in God, manifested through the virtue of hope, brings that deep, heartfelt assurance that all will work out right; God's way will prevail, and the end result will be even better than we could have imagined.

Directly linked to the faith we discussed earlier is the gift of hope. Packaged deeply inside every human being is a feeling of expectation, a feeling of anticipation, or a desire for a life offering greater fulfillment. Every individual is born with that intangible something, which yearns for a better existence, a better result, and a better something. Whether that expectation is for earthly material wealth, for honor or recognition, or for intangible, spiritual fulfillment, the yearning is as real as more tangible emotions such as hunger or fear.

> **Blessed is he whose help is the God of Jacob, whose hope is in the Lord his God. (Psalms 146:5)**

Throughout life, we are always looking forward to expectations of a better job, a better house, a better boss, a better church, and a better salary. As a matter of fact, those desires start very early in life as we express a desire for gifts, a desire for time with our fathers, a desire for toys, or a desire for a new bike. After a while, we begin to refer to that desire as *hope*. We hope for a boyfriend or a girlfriend, we hope we are accepted at a certain school, we hope our children are born healthy, or we hope our parents are compassionately cared for as they grow older.

We see that hope is an expectation of something yet to be fulfilled, something in the future, whether near term or long-term. Hope is something that implies that the desired result is out of our control and that somebody or something else will determine the outcome.

Hope is a wonderful human characteristic given as a gift from God and is a vital survival mode human trait. We see time and time again people who have lost all hope, people who have reached the end of the line. These people are destitute and void of any joy. They have lost that feeling of joyful expectation, of looking forward to a future of improved well-being and happiness. We see this in people who suffer in almost all forms of depression. Their faces and demeanor display emptiness, hopelessness, a complete inability to see any possibility of things getting better, or to see a brighter day tomorrow. They see no way out and nothing looks right or positive. Put another way, they have no hope. Nothing gives them a reason for going on living.

> **Find rest, O my soul, in God alone; my hope comes from him. He alone is my rock and my salvation; he is my fortress, I will not be shaken. My salvation and my honor depend on God; he is my mighty rock, my refuge. Trust in him at all times, O people; pour out your hearts to him, for God is our refuge. (Psalms 62:5–8)**

We as Christians have a better perspective. We have a hope in a better tomorrow, a better tomorrow spent in eternity with our Lord and Savior. Our hope is not founded on earthly matters or possessions. Our hope rests not on the vagaries of manmade goods or rewards. Riches mean nothing to us, except the riches we know we will inherit after this life is over.

> **When a wicked man dies, his hope perishes; all he expected from his power comes to nothing. (Proverbs 11:7)**

Hope is real and exists in every human being. But hope comes alive in our hearts when we come to the Lord amid all life's anxieties and let Him be the direction for our lives. Bringing your cares to God releases all the power and positiveness of hope. You will see life in a new light. The darkness of the road ahead will light up and pathways for your future will manifest.

> **Show me your ways, O LORD; teach me your paths. Guide me in your truth and teach me, for you are God my Savior. And my hope is in you all day long. (Psalms 25:4–5)**

> **But now, Lord, what do I look for? My hope is in you. (Psalms 39:7)**

> **No one whose hope is in you will ever be put to shame. (Psalms 25:3)**

> **But the eyes of the Lord are on those who fear him, on those whose hope is in his unfailing love. (Psalms 33:18)**

> **Remember your word to your servant, for you have given me hope. (Psalms 119:49)**

Jeremiah helps us remember what God has to say about all those who put their trust in God:

> **For I know the plans I have for you, declares the LORD, plans to prosper you and not to harm you, plans to give you hope and a future. (Jeremiah 29:11)**

Then Paul has these uplifting words:

> **And hope does not disappoint us, because God has poured out his love into our hearts by the Holy Spirit, whom he has given us. (Romans 5:5)**

> **For everything that was written in the past was written to teach us, so that through endurance and the encouragement of the Scriptures we might have hope. (Romans 15:4)**

Summarizing this short treatise on hope, Dr. Richard Powell of McGregor Baptist Church in Ft. Myers, Florida, said it best during one of his sermons in 2009 when he said, "We as Christians win! At the end of the 'game' we win!"

CHAPTER 3

Love and Compassion

The Lord is compassionate and gracious, slow to anger, abounding in love. (Psalms 103:8)

As a father has compassion on his children, so the Lord has compassion on those who fear him. (Psalms 103:13)

God has shown throughout our lives that He loves us and holds us in the palm of His hand. Love is probably the most powerful force known to mankind. Surely, it was God's first desire that we should exist on earth in a loving relationship with Him and live in a loving relationship with those around us. Our fall from grace changed all that. In committing the first sin, Adam and Eve showed that their love was not fully centered on God. With their free will, they chose to put their material desires ahead of the love of God. The special bond that God set for them was broken, and ever since, mankind has lived with that broken relationship.

God has continually commanded us to express and practice that love and compassion for our fellow human beings. God went to the ultimate expression of love by laying down the life of His only begotten Son for us to show He loved us and cherished us. But time and time again, we revert to our old sinful ways and go back to those selfish human desires and temptations.

But as soon as they were at rest, they again did what was evil in your sight. Then you abandoned them to the hand

11

of their enemies so that they ruled over them. And when they cried out to you again, you heard from heaven, and in your compassion you delivered them time after time. (Nehemiah 9:28)

As we will mention several times throughout this treatise, life will bring pains and sorrows. Life will bring disappointments and frustrations. In most cases, those setbacks will involve the actions of others—of friends, of children, of coworkers, and of neighbors. Yes, and you will have fellow Christians bring hurt and injury to you.

Yet God has commanded us to love those who hurt us, to love those who ridicule us, and to love those who aggravate an already painful situation. As Jesus said in Matthew 5:44:

Love your enemies and pray for those who persecute you.

The true mark of a Christ-centered person is when you can turn the other cheek and forgive those who have pained you, who have betrayed your confidence, those who have mocked you, or stolen from you. It takes a real act of courage and willpower to forgive and forget. That is exactly the lesson Christ taught throughout his ministry.

Hatred stirs up dissension, but love covers over all wrongs. (Proverbs 10:12)

Forgiveness is a difficult character trait. It does not naturally spring from a self-centered heart. Forgiveness needs nurturing and training. It needs practice and honing. Our natural, sin-centered impulse is to get even when we are under attack. We feel the need for a protective device, to swing back, to return the favor. Our character has been wounded, and we feel the urge to repay the insult. But Jesus did not do that. He turned the other cheek when he said:

I tell you, not seven times, but seventy-seven times. (Matthew 18:22)

A kindhearted woman gains respect, but ruthless men gain only wealth. A kind man benefits himself, but a cruel man brings trouble on himself. (Proverbs 11:16–17)

The love that we show our fellow man should be evidenced by compassion and understanding. The life of a Christian should exemplify an attitude of caring, understanding, and patience. The modern world teaches us not to become emotionally involved in the needs and cares of other people. They say we need to look out for ourselves and keep number one in mind. Never was that the attitude of Christ throughout his ministry. Jesus bent down, went out of his way, cared, and was concerned for those destitute and downtrodden. Compassion was the hallmark of his ministry and his actions.

Let love and faithfulness never leave you; bind them around your neck, write them on the tablet of your heart. Then you will win favor and a good name in the sight of God and man. (Proverbs 3:3–4)

If your enemy is hungry, give him food to eat; if he is thirsty, give him water to drink. In doing this, you will heap burning coals on his head, and the Lord will reward you. (Proverbs 25:21–22)

The modern world has taught us that lifetime success is found in the toys and material possessions we collect. All of life's measurements seem built around a secular tabulation of property values, investments, square footage of homes, size of boats, and number of cars. As you would expect, the modern world does not keep a tally of compassionate acts or extensions of love. There is no "America's 500 Richest" list tallied for acts of love and kindness, and there is no list of "Forbes 100 Most Compassionate Human Beings." But you can rest assured that God knows and has a record of how we treat our fellow human beings and how we express our love and compassion for those less privileged.

Practicing love and compassion takes practice. As we said, our natural, sinful nature does not make us naturally compassionate. We need to seek this fruit of the Spirit through prayer and meditation. We need to ask

God for a tender heart and a caring spirit. Then we need to ask God for the patience and temperament that is essential for a loving attitude. We also need to

- ask God to help us forget the hurts and wrongs done to us;
- seek God's will for our lives and ask Him to impart on us the Christ-like love in relations to our fellow man;
- be open to opportunities for practicing compassion;
- proactively reach out to offer love and compassion to those who are feeling pain and depression;
- encourage others to open their hearts to a better understanding of the power of love and compassion; and
- give unselfishly of our newfound gift and proclaim it in every activity we engage in.

Look around you every day. As you drive to work, take note of those less fortunate, those without the gifts you have been granted. Opportunities abound for the practice of love. Those housed in mental institutions need compassion. Those from your church who are bedridden or those in a hospital for extended stays need attention. Those elderly housed in care facilities need someone to show a little bit of love. Those sight-impaired people need someone to take them for a walk in the fresh spring air.

Make an effort to express the tender heart that goes hand in hand with the Christian life. It will bring you joy and will honor God in the process.

CHAPTER 4

Prayer

If I had cherished sin in my heart, the Lord would not have listened; but God has surely listened and heard my voice in prayer. Praise be to God, who has not rejected my prayer or withheld his love from me! (Psalms 66: 18–20)

If there had been any single behavior we wished we had practiced even more faithfully and with even more intensity, it was prayer. Oh, be sure we prayed regularly. We prayed for the Lord's blessings and for our needs, not our wants. We prayed in secret, and we prayed in good times as well as in bad. We prayed for the health and needs of others. We prayed for our governmental leaders. We prayed for our families, for our children, and for our parents. We prayed for our church, its leaders, its pastors, and its staff.

Over the years, we came to learn that Christians should be in constant prayer with God. No matter where you are or what you are doing, you need to be in constant prayer with God. Prayer is talking with God, prayer is communion with Him, and prayer is a bond with Him.

When we were young, we learned that prayer was the way of saying thank you to God for His blessings. We thanked Him for the daily gifts, the food, and the other necessities of life He so graciously had given us. Somewhere along the line, the practice of regular, intimate prayer slowly drifted from our lives. We got busy and preoccupied with matters of the world. Pressures of daily living crowded out the spiritual. We just plain forgot to pray. Other immediate matters muscled into our schedules and priority lists. Time deadlines never seemed to permit time for prayer. We never gave it a second thought that it should have been, and needed to be, the most central part of our life each hour of every day.

Never had we been so derelict in any faith practice than in our practice of prayer. For far too many years, prayer was a before bedtime duty and generally uttered before meals. Prayer was not an active part of our everyday life. We did not go humbly and faithfully to God in communication and supplication as He had so pleadingly asked and commanded us to do.

In practicing our Christian faith, we far too often relegated prayer to a formality. We tucked it neatly into a worship service, recited a repetition of meaningless clichés, and moved to the next item in the program without hardly ever thinking of what was said, let alone whom it was said to. Perhaps we were not alone.

Yet, going to the Word of God, the Lord is very specific in His commands to bring our burdens, our cares, and our needs to Him in prayer. There is probably no other command or plea the Lord makes that can be so profitable to our lives, and your lives, and which is so rich to our well-being, than the practice and act of prayer. God instituted prayer as a way for us, His lovingly created children, to commune with Him any time of the day, anywhere on earth, and in any condition that we find ourselves.

He will respond to the prayer of the destitute; he will not despise their plea. (Psalms 102:17)

Yet, prayer, if not practiced faithfully and diligently, soon gravitates to a perfunctory insert at weddings and funerals, or invoked at times of national crisis and need. During our day, our country went through the horrifying September 11, 2001 terrorist attacks in New York, Washington DC, and Pennsylvania. The nation instinctively "got religion" and every politician reached out to their constituency, asking for the prayers and blessings of God at a time of national need. While it seemed a natural instinct to turn to God, little thought was given that up to this time, the thought of public prayer was of little or no use. During this moment of national tragedy we seemed so helpless, so alone, and so in need. Sadly, as this book is coming to a conclusion in 2012, our country seems to have once again become complacent about the public proclamation of prayer.

Jesus offered guidance on how we must pray when in Matthew 6:9–13 he said:

This then is how you should pray:

Our Father in heaven, hallowed be your name,
Your kingdom come, your will be done,
On earth as it is in heaven.
Give us today our daily bread.
Forgive us our debts, as we also have forgiven our debtors.
And lead us not into temptation, but deliver us from the
evil one.

Jesus goes on to say in the parable regarding the publican and the Pharisee:

To some who were confident of their own righteousness
and looked down on everybody else, Jesus told this parable:
Two men went up to the temple to pray, one a Pharisee and
the other a tax collector. The Pharisee stood up and prayed
about himself: "God, I thank you that I am not like other
men—robbers, evildoers, adulterers—or even like this tax
collector. I fast twice a week and give a tenth of all I get."
But the tax collector stood at a distance. He would not even
look up to heaven, but beat his breast and said, "God have
mercy on me, a sinner." I tell you that this man, rather than
the other, went home justified before God. For everyone
who exalts himself will be humbled, and he who humbles
himself will be exalted. (Luke 18:9–14)

Now here is a truly sobering thought. God already knows what you will ask for. He knows why you are standing there or kneeling there and what it is that brought you here. He already knows your problem, worry, concern, hurt, and need. He also knows the remedy, the cure, and the time it will be applied. But you don't, and you won't, until you come humbly to God and seek His help and direction.

But when you pray, go into your room, close the door and
pray to your Father, who is unseen. Then your Father, who
sees what is done in secret, will reward you. And when you
pray, do not keep on babbling like pagans, for they think
they will be heard because of their many words. Do not be

like them, for your Father knows what you need before you ask him. (Matthew 6:6–8)

Don't be troubled or dismayed when, after repeated and repeated and repeated prayer, the solution is not the way you envisioned. It seldom is. God's plan for your life is well developed and sure. Believe us when we say that God knows what is best. We can't count the number of times when we prayed so diligently for a response, a specific response to a situation, only to have the prayer unanswered, or not answered in the way we had wanted. In the end, it turned out for the best. Whether it was a job for ourselves, mates for our children, a decision at our church, or whatever, God knew best, and the ultimate result was even more glorious than what we had requested. But the result was nothing like what we had originally had in mind. God knew His plan and His plan was wonderful, glorious, and joyous. Yet, we had to wait on the Lord and let His will unfold. That is why Paul said:

Be joyful in hope, patient in affliction, faithful in prayer. (Romans 12:12)

Prayer is intended in more than times of need. Prayer is offered in times of success, in times of joy, and in times of great blessings. The beauty of prayer is that you can practice it anytime and anywhere. God is present and attentive. Prayer can be offered in time of need, in time of despair, in the loss of a job, in the loss of a perceived opportunity, and in the loss of loved ones. Prayer of thanksgiving can also be offered when you got that right job, when your children have blessed you with children, and when you have overcome a serious illness.

"Count your blessings, name them one by one, and it will surprise you what the Lord has done." Oh, the words from that beautiful song. And ever so true. Take the time to look at what the Lord has provided you and you will see that your life is filled with so many blessings that you cannot name them all. Show thanks for those blessings and come to the Lord in prayer with a grateful and thankful heart.

Your prayer is personal and private. God expects you and us to come to Him with a penitent yet grateful heart. Daily, consistent, and heart-centered prayer makes a statement. If we expect God to be there in bad times, we had better be with Him in good times. The Bible mentions prayer so often that we wondered how we had missed it for so long.

We close this chapter with just a few of those verses that reminded us of God's calling to us and to you. The promises are sure, no doubt about it. See what He's done for others and He'll do it for you. Just see how each of these verses speaks to the power, intimacy, and comfort of prayer.

Therefore let everyone who is godly pray to you while you may be found; surely when the mighty waters rise, they will not reach him. (Psalms 32:6)

David built an altar to the LORD there and sacrificed burnt offerings and fellowship offerings. Then the LORD answered prayer in behalf of the land, and the plague on Israel was stopped. (2 Samuel 24:25)

So we fasted and petitioned our God about this, and he answered our prayer. (Ezra 8:23)

**O Lord, let your ear be attentive to the prayer of this your servant and to the prayer of your servants who delight in revering your name. Give your servant success today by granting him favor in the presence of this man.
I was cupbearer to the king. (Nehemiah 1:11)**

He will respond to the prayer of the destitute; he will not despise their plea. (Psalms 102:17)

The Lord detests the sacrifice of the wicked, but the prayer of the upright pleases him. (Proverbs 15:8)

The Lord is far from the wicked but he hears the prayer of the righteous. (Proverbs 15:29)

If you believe, you will receive whatever you ask for in prayer. (Matthew 21:22)

Therefore I tell you, whatever you ask for in prayer, believe that you have received it, and it will be yours. (Mark 11:24)

Do not deprive each other except by mutual consent and for a time, so that you may devote yourselves to prayer. Then come together again so that Satan will not tempt you because of your lack of self-control. (1 Corinthians 7:5)

Do not be anxious about anything, but in everything, by prayer and petition, with thanksgiving, present your requests to God. (Philippians 4:6)

And the prayer offered in faith will make the sick person well; the Lord will raise him up. If he has sinned, he will be forgiven. Therefore confess your sins to each other and pray for each other so that you may be healed. The prayer of a righteous man is powerful and effective. (James 5:15–16)

You will pray to him, and he will hear you, and you will fulfill your vows. (Job 22:27)

Seek the Lord while he may be found; call on him while he is near. (Isaiah 55:6)

Before they call I will answer; while they are speaking I will hear. (Isaiah 65:24)

Pray continually. (1 Thessalonians 5:17)

I want men everywhere to lift up holy hands in prayer, without anger or disputing. (1 Timothy 2:8)

The prayer of a righteous man is powerful and effective. (James 5:16)

This is the confidence we have in approaching God: that if we ask anything according to his will, he hears us. And if we know that he hears us—whatever we ask—we know that we have what we asked of him. (1 John 5:14)

CHAPTER 5

Wisdom

> Let not the wise man boast of his wisdom or the strong man boast of his strength or the rich man boast of his riches, but let him who boasts boast about this: that he understands and knows me, that I am the Lord, who exercises kindness, justice and righteousness on earth, for in these I delight, declares the Lord. (Jeremiah 9:23–24)

How we dream of the opportunities to get rich if we were just smart enough. Fantasies of riches and splendors dance in our minds and fill us with headlong urges to command vast domains. We might long for insight into the workings of the stock market or the real estate market. Or if we could grasp the intricacies of the next wonder drug or mine the workings of the next lightning-speed computer chip, we could amass a fortune. With that knowledge, we would control vast sums of wealth and have power of untold value. We think just having enough smarts will get us all we crave in material goods and possessions and bring the happiness we all desire.

> Blessed is the man who finds wisdom, the man who gains understanding, for she is more profitable than silver and yields better returns than gold. She is more precious than rubies; nothing you desire can compare with her. Long life is in her right hand; in her left hand are riches and honor. Her ways are pleasant ways, and all her paths are peace. She is a tree of life to those who embrace her; those who lay hold of her will be blessed. (Proverbs 3:13–18)

Many people have gone to their graves chasing the ever-fleeting rainbow of fame and fortune. Many have built their entire lives on the pursuit of earthly knowledge and human understanding.

He who trusts in himself is a fool, but he who walks in wisdom is kept safe. (Proverbs 28:26)

My son, if you accept my words and store up my commands within you, turning your ear to wisdom and applying your heart to understanding, and if you call out for insight and cry aloud for understanding, and if you look for it as for silver and search for it as for hidden treasure, then you will understand the fear of the Lord and find the knowledge of God. (Proverbs 2:1–5)

Wisdom should be the hope and quest of every Christian. Those who deny the Lord and seek to rely on their own skill and knowledge flail away in darkness and despair at the frustrations of life and its meaning. Man was given intelligence and a brain to learn the essence of the world around him. God endowed man with the ability to study, diagnose, gather knowledge, and develop his talents and skills to better his condition in life and truly experience all the good and wonderful things in God's creation. And yet, there is a certain something that is lacking in mere knowledge that is so necessary to grasp the higher meaning of our Lord's will for our lives.

The ability to grasp the intent of any given situation or God's will for your life is to understand the difference between knowledge and wisdom. Read the story of Solomon's first important decision after he became king of Israel and you see true wisdom at work. In 1 Kings 3:16–28, Solomon reaches a decision that would not necessarily be the first remedy that jumps forth in most people's minds. Solomon understood the natural instincts of a mother and the love of a mother for her child—a mother will do anything to sustain the life of her child. Solomon knew that the real mother would come to the forefront when confronted with the possibility of immediate death to the remaining baby (her child). Is this wisdom or what!

In the book of Proverbs, we read what Solomon described as wisdom and the value it brings:

Get wisdom, get understanding; do not forget my words or swerve from them. Do not forsake wisdom, and she will protect you; love her, and she will watch over you. Wisdom is supreme; therefore get wisdom. Though it cost all you have, get understanding. (Proverbs 4:5–7)

Listen to advice and accept instruction, and in the end you will be wise. (Proverbs 19:20)

Throughout life, you will be called to make decisions of paramount importance. Whether decisions about your career, your children, your marriage, your home, your church, or whatever, wisdom will be needed. But wisdom does not come naturally; knowledge maybe, but not wisdom. We know from the Bible that God grants wisdom to those who seek it.

Brothers, think of what you were when you were called. Not many of you were wise by human standards; not many were influential; not many were of noble birth. But God chose the foolish things of the world to shame the wise; God chose the weak things of the world to shame the strong. He chose the lowly things of this world and the despised things—and the things that are not—to nullify the things that are, so that no one may boast before him. It is because of him that you are in Christ Jesus, who has become for us wisdom from God—that is, our righteousness, holiness and retention. Therefore, as it is written: "Let him who boasts boast in the Lord." (1 Corinthians 1:26–31)

Wisdom is the gift graciously given by God to those who have put their faith in Him and seek out His omnipotence to grant them the power to comprehend the true essence of life's mysteries.

The book of Proverbs is packed with references to the value of wisdom. Nowhere in the Bible are there so many wise and wonderful descriptions of wisdom displayed and pronounced. Those who call themselves Christians should value and cherish wisdom.

My son, preserve sound judgment and discernment, do not let them out of your sight; they will be life for you, an ornament

to grace your neck. Then you will go on your way in safety, and your foot will not stumble; when you lie down, you will not be afraid; when you lie down, your sleep will be sweet. Have no fear of sudden disaster or of the ruin that overtakes the wicked, for the Lord will be your confidence and will keep your foot from being snared. (Proverbs 3:21–26)

Wisdom is supreme; therefore get wisdom. Though it cost all you have, get understanding. Esteem her, and she will exalt you; embrace her, and she will honor you. (Proverbs 4:7–8)

Listen, my son, accept what I say, and the years of your life will be many. I guide you in the way of wisdom and lead you along straight paths. When you walk, your steps will not be hampered; when you run, you will not stumble. Hold on to instruction, do not let it go; guard it well, for it is your life. (Proverbs 4:10–13)

I love those who love me, and those who seek me find me. With me are riches and honor, enduring wealth and prosperity. My fruit is better than fine gold; what I yield surpasses choice silver. I walk in the way of righteousness, along the paths of justice, bestowing wealth on those who love me and making their treasuries full. (Proverbs 8:17–21)

Now then, my sons, listen to me; blessed are those who keep my ways. Listen to my instruction and be wise; do not ignore it. Blessed is the man who listens to me, watching daily at my doors, waiting at my doorway. For whoever finds me finds life and receives favor from the Lord. But whoever fails to find me harms himself; all who hate me love death. (Proverbs 8:32–36)

Wise men store up knowledge, but the mouth of a fool invites ruin. (Proverbs 10:14)

The heart of the discerning acquires knowledge; the ears of the wise seek it out. (Proverbs 18:15)

A humble spirit usually goes hand in hand with the person who possesses true wisdom. God used the humble, the outcasts, the uneducated, and the sinners of the day to build his church. Christ's followers were men of humble and simple backgrounds. Most were fishermen, men who made their livings with their hands from the sweat of their backs.

> **Where is the wise man? Where is the scholar? Where is the philosopher of this age? Has not God made foolish the wisdom of the world? For since in the wisdom of God the world through its wisdom did not know him, God was pleased through the foolishness of what was preached to save those who believe. (1 Corinthians 1:20–21)**

> **For the foolishness of God is wiser than man's wisdom, and the weakness of God is stronger than man's strength. (1 Corinthians 1:25)**

The true wise man and woman show their wisdom through their acts of faith and good deeds. All the degrees, certificates of merit or honoraria cannot hold a candle to the acts of love, peace, kindness, and mercy. So we leave you with the charge to pray for wisdom, as Solomon did. Pray that God gives you a spirit of love and compassion. That you are given the power to discern and understand, not just know and recount. As brother James said so beautifully:

> **Who is wise and understanding among you? Let him show it by his good life, by deeds done in humility that comes from wisdom. But if you harbor bitter envy and selfish ambition in your hearts, do not boast about it or deny the truth. Such "wisdom" does not come down from heaven but is earthly, unspiritual, of the devil. For where you have envy and selfish ambition, there you find disorder and every evil practice. But the wisdom that comes from heaven is first of all pure; then peace-loving, considerate, submissive, full of mercy and good fruit, impartial and sincere. Peacemakers who sow in peace raise a harvest of righteousness. (James 3:13–18)**

CHAPTER 6

Trust in the Lord

Trust in the Lord with all your heart and lean not on your own understanding; in all your ways acknowledge him, and he will make your paths straight. (Proverbs 3:5-6)

Uncertainty, fear, depression, doubt, hopelessness, and despair—all are human emotions that plague the human spirit. Every single day we feel the helplessness of life. Nothing seems to go right. Everything seems in turmoil. Wherever we turn, there seems to be no answer. The best efforts we put forward always seem to fall short. Our talents seem so helpless, and we never can seem to get it right.

Well, join the ranks of the countless millions upon millions who have experienced the same phenomena. History is filled with rulers, leaders, public officials, and just plain ordinary citizens who have struggled continuously with life only to see their efforts end in emptiness, failure, and despair. Such is the result of depending on your own efforts and your own knowledge. We struggle with our occupation, we struggle with family, and we struggle with the daily grind of life. We never seem to have enough money, talent, or endurance. Our efforts always seem to fall short, and we never seem to get to a point where we feel at rest.

Life has a way of making us feel helpless and alone. You will go through periods when purpose and dreams evaporate into nothingness and you just can't seem to find your way.

Once again, turn to the rich passages of scripture and see that God shows us the blessings He has in store for us if we trust in Him.

Trust in the Lord and do good; dwell in the land and enjoy safe pasture. Delight yourself in the Lord and he will give you the desires of your heart. (Psalms 37:3–4)

Commit to the Lord whatever you do, and your plans will succeed. (Proverbs 16:3)

Throughout our working life and child-rearing years, we found that every ten years or so, a new challenge seemed to appear. Whether vocation, relationships with each other, relationships with our church or our business associates, we just seemed to lose our way. Looking for a new job, or agonizing about the purchase of a new home, or making a family decision, became a difficult challenge. We just couldn't seem to find the answer.

Then we began to reach into the Word of God. How had we missed it so many times before? What was it that made these decisions so difficult? Why did we make the effort so difficult when God was there waiting for us to reach out to Him and seek His will?

If you make the Most High your dwelling—even the Lord, who is my refuge—then no harm will befall you, no disaster will come under your tent.

For he will command his angels concerning you to guard you in all your ways; they will lift you up in their hands, so that you will not strike your foot against a stone.

You will tread upon the lion and the cobra; you will trample the great lion and the serpent.

"Because he loves me," says the Lord, "I will rescue him; I will protect him, for he acknowledges my name. He will call upon me, and I will answer him; I will be with him in trouble, I will deliver him and honor him. With long life will I satisfy him and show him my salvation." (Psalms 91:9–16)

Looking back, we saw that the Lord provided us with our needs; our wants far too often got in the way. This little writing by Mary Stevenson says it all:

One night a man had a dream. He dreamed
he was walking along the beach with the LORD.

Across the sky flashed scenes from his life.
For each scene, he noticed two sets of
footprints in the sand: one belonging
to him, and the other to the LORD.

When the last scene of his life flashed before him,
he looked back at the footprints in the sand.

He noticed that many times along the path of
his life there was only one set of footprints.

He also noticed that it happened at the very
lowest and saddest times in his life.

This really bothered him and he
questioned the LORD about it:

"LORD, you said that once I decided to follow
you, you'd walk with me all the way.
But I have noticed that during the most
troublesome times in my life,
there is only one set of footprints.
I don't understand why when
I needed you most you would leave me."

The LORD replied:
"My son, my precious child,
I love you and I would never leave you.
During your times of trial and suffering,
when you see only one set of footprints,
it was then that I carried you."

If you do not believe that God created the world—human life and the astronomical wonders—then surely you'll never see His power to direct your destiny and your path through life. Trust in the Lord is founded on a firm foundation of faith. You must believe there is a God. You must believe He's a personal God who loves us so much that He sent His Son to die for us. Do you honestly, down in your heart, believe that God cares about you, knows your needs, and can affect human activity to sustain and care for His own?

God has proclaimed that there is a way that we can see fulfillment and experience enjoyment. The psalmist said it best when he said:

> **But let all who take refuge in you be glad; let them ever sing for joy. Spread your protection over them, that those who love your name may rejoice in you. For surely, O Lord, you bless the righteous; you surround them with your favor as with a shield. (Psalms 5:11–12)**

Emil Boniog, pastor at Life in Christ Church in California gave a very moving sermon on temptation and working through the trials of life. Read what he has to say in his message on "God Will Make A Way," from 1 Corinthians 10:13:

> Having Christ in your heart does not mean that you will no longer have problems. The Lord said it very plainly in John 16:33, "In this world you will have trouble." Christians and non-Christians will both encounter problems in this life.
> This morning I want us to consider one verse in particular, namely, 1 Cor. 10:13. It says, "No temptation has seized you except what is common to man. And God is faithful; he will not let you be tempted beyond what you can bear. But when you are tempted, he will also provide a way out so that you can stand up under it."
> I have yet to hear somebody say, "I have a big TEMPTATION in my life." We always say, "I have a big PROBLEM in my life." Your problem could be about your finances (you are on the verge of foreclosing your house), your job (you just got a job termination notice), your family (your son is taking drugs or

your daughter is going out with a married man or your spouse is threatening to divorce you), or about other areas of life. You may choose to call it stress, frustrations, mental anguish, crisis, or any other name. The fact is your problem is potentially a temptation to act against God's moral standards. It could be that you are tempted to cheat, to lie, to be mean, to hurt someone, and a variety of other unchristian reactions.

Today, I want us to see seven principles about TEMPTATION.

1. Temptation is "common to man." You say, "You don't understand. Nobody has it as bad as me." You're wrong. Everybody experiences some kind of temptation. Even the Lord Jesus Himself was tempted in all points (Heb. 4:15). The Lord was not exempted.

I want to make it clear that God does not tempt anyone in the sense of enticing to sin (James 1:13). However, he allows "trials" and "testing" in our life in order to strengthen our faith and to confirm our allegiance to Him.

2. Temptation is unique to "you."

You say, "You don't know my boss," or "You don't know my kids," or "You're not married to my wife." You're right about that. She is your wife, not mine. In a sense, it is unique to you. You yourself got into this problem. It's yours, not mine. But don't forget something. I have my own unique problem. What we share is the fact that we both have problems. We are in the same boat, so to speak. You have your mess and I have mine. What is common to us is the fact that we are both a mess. The point is, we have different weaknesses and different degrees of weakness, and God is dealing with us individually, according to our need. I may be weak in money matters, so God is testing me in this area with the view of strengthening me in this area. Your weakness may be in sexual matters, and so God is testing you in that area with the end in mind of making you stronger in resisting sexual temptations.

3. Temptation proves the faithfulness of God. "God is faithful" to Himself. He cannot deny Himself. In fact, "if we are faithless, He will remain faithful, for He cannot disown Himself" (2 Tim. 2:15). It is "godlike" (natural for God) for Him to act in love. He cannot but love just as light cannot keep itself from throwing light in a dark room. Paul says that the grace of God increases proportionate to the degree of sin (Romans 5:20). What he means is that the greater the sin the more grace is required. It is no excuse to sin as Paul is very careful to point out (Romans 6:1). It is simply the fact as, in the case of water, "water rises to its own level," as the old saying goes.

"God is faithful" also to His Word. This is an encouragement for us to know His Word because "there hath not failed one word of all his good promise" (1 Kings 8:56). Claim His promises. Trust His Word. Apply it on your circumstance. Eph. 6:17 says that the Word of God is the sword of the Spirit by which you can overcome and be victorious.

4. God will not allow you to be tempted "beyond what you can bear." God knows your strength. He knows what you can bear. If you are a "babe in Christ," like a Grade I teacher, He will only give you a Grade I test. Will you give your seven-year-old boy a fifty-pound bag of rice to carry? Of course not. So where in the world did you get the idea that God will allow a problem that is beyond your ability to carry? Are you better in fathering than God? Cease the thought.

5. Temptation is certain. Our text does not say "if" you are tempted, but rather "when" you are tempted. In other words, it's just a matter of when. Problems are sure to come. It's in the territory, so they say. The question is, are you ready? Do you know how to handle temptation? Do you know what the Word of God teaches about temptation? When are you going to prepare yourself?

6. "God will provide a way out." I think it is a mistake for us to pray, "God, I pray that you take this problem away," or "Lord, please spare me from trouble." It is true that the Lord teaches us

to pray, "Lead us not into temptation" (Matt. 6:13). I see that as a statement of truth that God does not lead into temptation, that is, He does not entice someone to sin.

I don't think our text is telling us to ask God to make a way around our problems. If you read the text right, you will see that you are already in the problem. "The way out" then is God's overpowering triumph and deliverance from the problem.

Don Moen wrote a song from which we borrowed the title of this message. Here are the lyrics of that heart-moving song:

> God will make a way,
> Where there seems to be no way
> He works in ways we cannot see
> He will make a way for me
> He will be my guide
> Hold me closely to His side
> With love and strength for each new day
> He will make a way, He will make a way.
> By a roadway in the wilderness, He'll lead me
> And rivers in the desert will I see
> Heaven and earth will fade
> But His Word will still remain
> He will do something new today.
> God will make a way,
> Where there seems to be no way
> He works in ways we cannot see
> He will make a way for me
> He will be my guide
> Hold me closely to His side
> With love and strength for each new day
> He will make a way, He will make a way.

7. God will help you to stand up under temptation.
The moment you decide to trust God, He will infuse His strength through the Holy Spirit so that you can say with Paul, "I can do all things through Jesus Christ who strengthens me" (Phil. 4:13). He will help you to go through the problem with

peace in your heart and a song on your lips. You will be like the three Jewish young men who were thrown into the furnace of fire by the decree of Nebuchadnezzar. But you have to have the attitude of those young men who boldly proclaimed to the king, "If you throw us into the blazing furnace, the God we serve is able to save us from the furnace. He will save us from your power, O king. But even if God does not save us, we want you, O king, to know this: We will not serve your gods or worship the gold statue you have set up."

To you, our blessed children and grandchildren, know that God can make a way. Every human breath, action, and event is under His control. But you must trust Him and choose His deliverance.

> **Though the fig tree does not bud and there are no grapes on the vines, though the olive crop fails and the fields produce no food, though there are no sheep in the pen and no cattle in the stalls, yet I will rejoice in the Lord, I will be joyful in God my Savior. (Habbakukk 3:17–18)**

> **The Lord your God is with you, he is mighty to save. He will take great delight in you, he will quiet you with his love, he will rejoice over you with singing. (Zephaniah 3:17)**

Trust in the Lord as the first option, not the last. Just look at the patriarchs of old and the trust they put in God during times of trial and adversity. Think of Moses, Gideon, David, Abraham, Elijah, and Solomon. Then think of Joshua when he had to contend with standing strong in the face of what appeared to be insurmountable odds in conquering the promised land. In the end, let us all join in unison with Joshua and say:

> **Now fear the Lord and serve him with all faithfulness . . . But as for me and my household, we will serve the Lord. (Joshua 24:14–15)**

CHAPTER 7

The Bible

For the Word of God is living and active. Sharper than any double-edged sword, it penetrates even to dividing soul and spirit, joints and marrow; it judges the thoughts and attitudes of the heart. Nothing in all creation is hidden from God's sight. Everything is uncovered and laid bare before the eyes of him to whom we must give account. (Hebrews 4:12–13)

No book should travel with you more throughout your life, and no other book should be, or will be, your most trusted companion than the Bible.

Over the years, we received as gifts, or purchased for our own use, an untold number of Bibles. Each has had a place of special remembrance in our hearts. Even to this day, we still have the Bible given to us by Pastor Dr. Elton Holtrop who married us on April 27, 1962. When we leaf through its pages, we are reminded of the faithfulness God had shown us so long ago. Our lives went in directions we never imagined when we first set out on the path of marital union. We traveled to places we never expected, met so many people in the United States and foreign lands, served in more churches, kingdom and community organizations, and met more political leaders than even our wildest dreams could have ever imagined. We grew in knowledge and understanding of the most esoteric sciences. We collected more books than we ever could have read on subjects that to this day are as confusing as ever. But most importantly, and through it all, the Bible was there, always faithful and full of God-inspired instructions for living a life free from fear, in step with God's purpose, and seeing the blessings that go with a life focused on honoring His will.

Yet, as frail, sin-prone human beings, too many times we failed to remember the lessons God had for us in His Word. Too often, we were blindly caught up in the pursuit of worldly goals. Too many times, we lost our bearings and found ourselves hopelessly off course. What greater joys we could have experienced, and pains we could have avoided, if we had faithfully and religiously turned in those times of strife to the Lord's Word and practiced what is so clearly, easily, and lovingly stated in His commands.

The Bible is not a book to be read infrequently, put on a shelf, and then read once again when time permits or when life's trials overtake us. No, the Bible is to be read with regularity and with purpose in good times and in bad. No simple, casual reading of the Bible can bring out its truths or its lessons of life. Regular and critical systematic reading is crucial. Repetition is good and wholesome. Only then do you begin to see the power and richness of the words and thoughts. Then the purpose shines through, bringing us into full harmony and resonance with God's stated will for our lives, and prepares us to meet the challenges on the road ahead.

The Bible is sometimes a very specific how-to manual from the Author and Giver of life. At other times, it is more general and figurative, yet still appealing to our God-given common sense. Its pages are filled with the secrets of the world and ways to enjoy life to the fullest. Its messages offer hope to the weary and peace to the afflicted. The joys of life become available to us when we practice the lessons of old. However, do not forget that our primary mission and purpose here on earth is to worship and please God. He expects our complete loyalty and devotion. While events of the day-to-day world have a way of elbowing the Lord out of our lives, the Lord will remind us promptly and clearly about our wayward behavior. It is here that the Bible offers the way to Godly behavior. Salvation is offered to all, and the good news for obtaining that salvation is manifested clearly and openly in His Word.

The Bible is the living Word of God sent to help guide mankind—to you our dear grandchildren, to us as grandparents, and to the countless millions who came before us and who will come after us. We fell from His love and favor when we, through our first father and mother (Adam and Eve), betrayed God and opted for the curious and lucrative lusts of the world. Yet God loved us so much that He gave us a roadmap that showed the way back to His love and favor. The Bible is that roadmap. God loved us so dearly and faithfully that He gave His Son as a sacrifice for our sins and ransomed us back to freedom and eternity with Him.

To get the roadmap to work for you, you must be sure to study it faithfully. Pay special attention to its directions and warning signs, to its promises and hope, and to its comfort and love. The Bible is, without doubt, a message from God as much to you and to us as it was to the children of Israel and all God's people over the ages. It is powerful. It is truthful. It cuts right to the heart of every facet of life and leaves nothing to doubt. Read once again how the writer in Hebrews puts it:

> **For the word of God is living and active. Sharper than any double-edged sword, it penetrates even to dividing soul and spirit, joints and marrow: it judges the thoughts and attitudes of the heart. Nothing in all creation is hidden from God's sight. Everything is uncovered and laid bare before the eyes of him to whom we must give account. (Hebrews 4:12–13)**

The Word goes right to the heart of every situation in life. Just read the book of Proverbs. You soon realize that every ailment, trial, pain, and anguish befalling you today existed centuries ago. We sure saw that in our lives. God's Word is magnificent in bringing to the forefront the remedies for living a life under His care. With sin in the world, none of us is free from the hurts and pains of the sin-filled hearts and desires of man. Through a thorough study of the Word of God, we can be armed, prepared, and able to deal with adversities when trials arise. The Lord tells us that we need to flee from sin and arm ourselves for battle with evil. As scripture tells us:

> **Finally, be strong in the Lord and in his mighty power. Put on the full armor of God so that you can take your stand against the devil's schemes. For our struggle is not against flesh and blood, but against the rulers, against the authorities, against the powers of this dark world and against the spiritual forces of evil in the heavenly realms. (Ephesians 6:10–12)**

To think that the Word of God, the foundation for God's people more than two thousand years ago, is still with us today. The Bible is the most popular read book in print. It has withstood attacks and smears. It has prevailed through times of turmoil and national despair. And it has withstood the attacks of intellectuals who have sought to undermine its authenticity and historicity. The Bible survived every attack and onslaught, and it continues to stand as a pillar of strength in a time of need.

Yet reading His Word is only half the job. *Living* the message is what God had in mind. And living that message is as true for you today as it was in our day. You need to read the Bible actively and passionately to fully appreciate its power and promise, and then apply those lessons in your daily life.

You can be sure that many around you will mock the Word of God. You will be called to stand strong in your faith when for the moment everything and everyone seems to be working against your beliefs and your principles. To the unbelieving, the Word is nothing more than a relic out of the caves of antiquity. The unbelieving see the Word as an essay from antiquity based on a level equal to the works of Plato, Socrates, or Muhammad. The unbelieving see the Word as a meaningless collection of histories and morality lessons that have little or no practical application in today's educated and enlightened world. While interesting and thought provoking, the Bible is seen as nothing more than one culture's approach to life and the history of how it came to be.

Well, just don't believe it! God's Word is alive with truth and meaning. God knew that man would forever reject His teachings and His precepts. But you, our blessed children and grandchildren, are not just any ordinary persons—none of you. You have been raised in the faith and the knowledge of a loving God and His Son, Jesus Christ. Through this upbringing, you have been given a blessing far greater than any earthly riches can impart. For through knowing the God of Creation and of Life, you have knowledge of and have access to the most wonderful support system in the world. Never lose it, and never give up reading God's Word. Turn to it every day. Your worries and threats of today are nothing new. Your hope and comfort will be found in God's Word. You have been trained to seek it out in times of personal struggle and pain.

It is never too late to start down the path of faithful Bible reading. Set aside a time every day. Do it early in the morning, or first thing at work, or take an hour every night. Stick to the schedule. If you are traveling, read it on an airplane. Read it in an airport. Read it in a hotel room. After only a week, you will find that the practice of regular reading has become a habit, and the habit becomes a tradition, a tradition that is wholesome and good. Then you will find that faithful reading will lead to faithful praying, and faithful praying will lead to a greater desire to read more. In no time, you will find yourself communicating with God in ways you never thought possible. You will see God's blessings in a new light and will know that your continued well-being is a blessing from God, and you will find comfort and solace in the shelter of His care.

Faithful Bible reading brings out answers and solutions you never knew existed in the Word. You will see the power of the Word jumping out in a living way that will touch you personally and meaningfully. It will speak to your immediate needs. It will heal the hurts you are feeling. You will find joy at reading how God was at the right moment for His people when times were difficult. Watch how God is there in your lives in the same loving and miraculous ways as He was with the believers of old. Then you will begin to see how you are armed with wisdom and understanding to reach out to others who are struggling with life's pains and tragedies as well.

Oh, how we wish we had known (or at least fully comprehended) this power earlier in our lives. But praise God, we found it and began to joy in its blessings, as we grew stronger in the understanding and discernment of the biblical truths. Now in our later years, we are all consumed in learning more and more about God's faithfulness and healing power. The Bible governs every facet of our lives today—our worship, our jobs, our family relationships, our friend relationships, our church relationship, our sicknesses, and on and on.

To you, our children and grandchildren, and to others who may be reading this work, grab hold of the Word and cherish it. Don't let time pass while you wander around in a field of hopeless pursuit. God knows your needs. He has given His Word to lead you to Him, to give you a map to His eternal rest. The Word will lead you to God, and along the way, will multiply your blessings in abundance while on earth.

> **Oh, how I love your law! I mediate on it all day long. Your commands make me wiser than my enemies, for they are ever with me. I have more insight than all my teachers, for I meditate on your statutes. I have more understanding than the elders, for I obey your precepts. I have kept my feet from every evil path so that I might obey your word. I have not**

departed from your laws, for you yourself have taught me. How sweet are your words to my taste, sweeter than honey to my mouth! I gain understanding from your precepts; therefore I hate every wrong path. (Psalms 119:97–104)

Your word is a lamp to my feet and a light for my path. (Psalms 119:105)

The Bible serves many purposes, and its objectives can be summarized as follows:

- The Bible firmly establishes your faith in one God: the Creator of all things—the Giver of Life, the Ruler of the world
- The Bible tells how God loves His people and leads them back to Him, how He nurtures them, how He guides them, how He instructs them, and how He disciplines them
- The Bible shows how God hates sin and will not protect even those He loves from the consequences of sin
- The Bible shows how God so loved His creation that He sent His Son to die, once and for all, for the sins of the people—even you and us
- The Bible shows how we can find eternal life, after this life here on earth is over, through Christ our Savior

Oh, so very, very simple, so easy to attain, and yet so fleeting to the masses. But be sure you do not follow the masses. God raised you in His knowledge for your salvation. Do not let that slip away.

In your Bible study, don't worry about which translation you use. In our time, we grew up with the King James Version. Then numerous other translations came on the scene and many churches (including those we attended) settled on the New International Version. We also felt equally at ease with the Living Bible translation, which is considered a paraphrase. The New American Standard Version is an excellent translation as well, along with the New King James Version, which we are using in our church today. No matter the translation, make a point of studying the scripture faithfully. Take it with you always. Practice its teachings with fervor. Seek out its testimony and carry it with you where life takes you. As Timothy says:

All Scripture is God-breathed and is useful for teaching, rebuking, correcting and training in righteousness, so that the man of God may be thoroughly equipped for every good work. (2 Timothy 3:16–17)

You learned a little song when you were young. That song is so beautiful and full of truth. It is a testimony even in our later years. It goes like this:

> The B-I-B-L-E
> Yes, that's the book for me
> I stand alone on the Word of God
> The B-I-B-L-E

Keep your commitment strong to study the Word, stay faithful in your reading, and never depart from its paths. God so lovingly desires you seek after Him and follow His ways. From us, your grandparents, we ask you, or even plead with you, to quest for God's Word.

CHAPTER 8

The Ten Commandments

> So if you faithfully obey the commands I am giving you today—to love the Lord your God and to serve him with all your heart and with all your soul—then I will send rain on your land in its season, both autumn and spring rains, so that you may gather in your grain, new wine and oil. I will provide grass in the fields for your cattle, and you will eat and be satisfied. (Deuteronomy 11:13–15)

We now turn to the bedrock of our personal faith, the faith of our parents and grandparents, and the very foundation of our own personal Christian values. The Ten Commandments given by God to the Israelites almost four thousand years ago were not only commands with promise to God's then chosen people, but the same commandments formed the foundation of how we, in our daily lives, chose to practice, and did practice, our devotion and love for God.

Once the children of Israel were safely across the Red Sea, free from the bondage of their Egyptian masters, the Lord prepared a new nation, a new life for His chosen people. For more than four hundred years, the Israelites lived with and governed themselves by Egyptian traditions and values. Those values and culture did not hold the God of Creation at the center of its faith. God knew that He needed to prepare and mold His people in the way of their fathers.

Once the people were safely out of reach from the Egyptians, God established a framework of societal rules, laws, and behaviors that the new nation would follow as they began a life in the way of the Lord. With a multitude of daily rituals and behaviors spelled out for the people, leaders, and priests, God established a foundation for wholesome living and behavior upon which the newly founded nation could begin. After all, the people would have to be assured they lived in a clean environment free from disease. They needed to be educated in ways that assured accordance with God and His ways. God wanted His people to live a life of devotion and dedication to His will.

God saw that His people needed a standard by which they could live in this world. When sin entered the heart of man, every evil desire and drive would, and could, overtake the human race. Needing a standard by which man could live in harmony with God, He created the Ten Commandments. The commandments made it clear as to what was considered acceptable and wholesome behavior.

The Ten Commandments set out in exceedingly clear and concise terms those behaviors that were to serve as the foundation of Godly living. The commandments established a framework of obedience to God and respect for fellow humans. The commandments were a foundation that peoples forever could follow and live in harmony with God and carry on a civil and loving existence among one another.

First, take a moment and read each command. Notice the clarity and succinctness. Cherish the value implicit in each one.

And God spoke all these words: I am the Lord your God, who brought you out of Egypt, out of the land of slavery.

- **You shall have no other gods before me.**
- **You shall not make for yourself an idol in the form of anything in heaven above or on the earth beneath or in the waters below. You shall not bow down to them or worship them; for I, the Lord your God, am a jealous God, punishing the children for the sin of the fathers to the third and fourth generation of those who hate me, but showing love to a thousand generations of those who love me and keep my commandments.**
- **You shall not misuse the name of the Lord your God, for the Lord will not hold anyone guiltless who misuses his name.**
- **Remember the Sabbath day by keeping it holy. Six days you shall labor and do all your work, but the seventh**

> day is a Sabbath to the Lord your God. On it you shall not do any work, neither you, nor your son or daughter, nor your manservant or maidservant, nor your animals, nor the alien within your gates. For in six days the Lord made the heavens and the earth, the sea, and all that is in them, but he rested on the seventh day. Therefore the Lord blessed the Sabbath day and made it holy.
>
> - Honor your father and your mother, so that you may live long in the land the Lord your God is giving you.
> - You shall not murder.
> - You shall not commit adultery.
> - You shall not steal.
> - You shall not give false testimony against your neighbor.
> - You shall not covet your neighbor's house. You shall not covet your neighbor's wife, or his manservant or maidservant, his ox or donkey, or anything that belongs to your neighbor. (Exodus 20:1–17)

These commandments are as applicable and meaningful today as ever before. On first reading, it becomes obvious that these commandments describe sins, vices, and evil cravings just as prevalent and rampant in today's world as they were in that of the patriarchs. God knew mankind would wrestle with sins that would recur generation after generation. There is truly nothing new about theft, about adultery, about jealousy, about lying, or about putting other gods before the God of Creation. They existed then and they surely exist now.

But how our lives get misdirected and disoriented. We are caught up in the affairs of daily life, the pressure to succeed, the urge to be recognized, and the desire to be loved. Then there is the overarching urge to possess, possess as much, as big, as expensive, as showy or as glamorous as anything that money can buy. Then the trouble begins.

The passionate urge to possess, and to possess material earthly possessions, leads us to a craving desire for money. It's money, largely, that is the mechanism to fulfill all those earthly needs. Money sets us apart from the rest of the world. Money gives us the feeling of importance, power, and control. Then, very shortly thereafter, that very quest for money leads us to violations of a whole host of the other commands. Not too far down the road, the breaking of these commands and precepts leads to an ever-greater need for more and more. Before you know it, we have become a slave to the very thing that we felt would be a slave to us and would satisfy us the most.

Life's joys are found in the things of God and nowhere else. Your life will be as full and enjoyable as you conform to the will of God. That promise is sure and God's precepts and commands are clear. No ambiguities, no misunderstandings, and no fogginess about it! Moreover, the promise is as clear as 1-2-3. You could even go so far as to put it into a scientific formula—*Obedience=Happiness.*

The psalmist says in Psalm 119:

Your statutes are wonderful; therefore I obey them. The unfolding of your words gives light; it gives understanding to the simple. I open my mouth and pant, longing for your commands. Turn to me and have mercy on me, as you always do to those who love your name. Direct my footsteps according to your word; let no sin rule over me. Redeem me from the oppression of men, that I may obey your precepts. Make your face shine upon your servant and teach me your decrees. Streams of tears flow from my eyes, for your law is not obeyed. (Psalms 119:129–136)

Great peace have they who love your law, and nothing can make them stumble. (Psalms 119:165)

You will hear from many so-called friends, colleagues, or neighbors that today's world is different. "We're not living in our grandparents' day." "Today's world is a new paradigm." "The old ways just don't work today." "The people of old just didn't have the pressures we have today."

Don't believe it! Don't believe any of it for one moment! In your time, as it was in ours, there will be people who will try to steal, murder, lie, covet the other sex, desire what you have, break your heart, deceive you, steal your personal belongings, and break the law to get it. These sins are as basic and as real today as they were thousands of years ago. The heart of man is as evil in its intent today as it ever was.

Don't let anyone fool you. These commands are as relevant today as they have ever been, because man's sins are as prevalent as ever. There is nothing new in this world, as the writer of Ecclesiastes says:

What has been will be again, what has been done will be done again; there is nothing new under the sun. (Ecclesiastes 1:9)

These laws are God's message to us in response to the fall of our first parents. We are as guilty and prone to committing those very sins that got Satan thrown out of heaven and those very sins Satan used to pollute the world. Therefore, God chose to give us in very clear, concise, and understandable language what we must do to continue in His grace. These commandments transcend cultural and national borders. Go to any foreign land. The people of those countries suffer the same crimes and failings as we do in America. Man's basic depravity is universal.

God gave and still gives us these commands for a purpose. That purpose is to allow us to live in His holiness and joy as He had planned when we were first created. The promise of a blessed life is real; rewards beyond comparison are there to be had. That's what God desired and still desires for us. When you begin to practice these commands faithfully, you begin to see the true joy of living. We experienced this repeatedly. We shared in God's riches when we were faithful to His ways and commands. God blessed us beyond our wildest imaginations when we sought His will. But when we strayed and disobeyed, trouble soon ensued and heavy prices were paid. Space does not permit telling how many times we paid the price and in what ways, but believe us, we paid it, and we knew it.

Now all has been heard; here is the conclusion of the matter: Fear God and keep his commandments, for this is the whole duty of man. (Ecclesiastes 12:13)

Righteous are you, O Lord, and your laws are right. The statutes you have laid down are righteous; they are fully trustworthy. (Psalms 119:137–138)

Look at your life and make an honest assessment. Have you abided by these commands? Have you kept every one? The answer is no! For no one has. When you come to understand that, you are then prepared to go to the Lord and ask His forgiveness and begin anew. Your life will start anew, filled with joy and exciting rewards.

Take the time to read Deuteronomy 28. It says it all about the blessings at hand, but it is also a warning about the results of disobedience. Read it carefully and grasp the surety of the promise. The blessings are to be had, but the price of disobedience is also sure.

Blessings for Obedience

¹**If you fully obey the LORD your God and carefully follow all his commands I give you today, the LORD your God will set you high above all the nations on earth. ²All these blessings will come upon you and accompany you if you obey the LORD your God: ³You will be blessed in the city and blessed in the country. ⁴The fruit of your womb will be blessed, and the crops of your land and the young of your livestock—the calves of your herds and the lambs of your flocks. ⁵Your basket and your kneading trough will be blessed. ⁶You will be blessed when you come in and blessed when you go out.**

⁷**The LORD will grant that the enemies who rise up against you will be defeated before you. They will come at you from one direction but flee from you in seven.**

⁸**The LORD will send a blessing on your barns and on everything you put your hand to. The LORD your God will bless you in the land he is giving you.**

⁹**The LORD will establish you as his holy people, as he promised you on oath, if you keep the commands of the LORD your God and walk in his ways.**

¹⁰**Then all the peoples on earth will see that you are called by the name of the LORD, and they will fear you.**

¹¹The LORD will grant you abundant prosperity—in the fruit of your womb, the young of your livestock and the crops of your ground—in the land he swore to your forefathers to give you.

¹²The LORD will open the heavens, the storehouse of his bounty, to send rain on your land in season and to bless all the work of your hands. You will lend to many nations but will borrow from none.

¹³The LORD will make you the head, not the tail. If you pay attention to the commands of the LORD your God that I give you this day and carefully follow them, you will always be at the top, never at the bottom.

¹⁴Do not turn aside from any of the commands I give you today, to the right or to the left, following other gods and serving them.

Curses for Disobedience

¹⁵However, if you do not obey the LORD your God and do not carefully follow all his commands and decrees I am giving you today, all these curses will come upon you and overtake you:

¹⁶You will be cursed in the city and cursed in the country.

¹⁷Your basket and your kneading trough will be cursed.

¹⁸The fruit of your womb will be cursed, and the crops of your land, and the calves of your herds and the lambs of your flocks.

¹⁹You will be cursed when you come in and cursed when you go out.

[20]The LORD will send on you curses, confusion and rebuke in everything you put your hand to, until you are destroyed and come to sudden ruin because of the evil you have done in forsaking him. [21]The LORD will plague you with diseases until he has destroyed you from the land you are entering to possess. [22]The LORD will strike you with wasting disease, with fever and inflammation, with scorching heat and drought, with blight and mildew, which will plague you until you perish. [23]The sky over your head will be bronze, the ground beneath you iron. [24]The LORD will turn the rain of your country into dust and powder; it will come down from the skies until you are destroyed.

[25]The LORD will cause you to be defeated before your enemies. You will come at them from one direction but flee from them in seven, and you will become a thing of horror to all the kingdoms on earth. [26]Your carcasses will be food for all the birds of the air and the beasts of the earth, and there will be no one to frighten them away. [27]The LORD will afflict you with the boils of Egypt and with tumors, festering sores and the itch, from which you cannot be cured. [28]The LORD will afflict you with madness, blindness and confusion of mind. [29]At midday you will grope about like a blind man in the dark. You will be unsuccessful in everything you do; day after day you will be oppressed and robbed, with no one to rescue you.

[30]You will be pledged to be married to a woman, but another will take her and ravish her. You will build a house, but you will not live in it. You will plant a vineyard, but you will not even begin to enjoy its fruit. [31]Your ox will be slaughtered before your eyes, but you will eat none of it. Your donkey will be forcibly taken from you and will not be returned. Your sheep will be given to your enemies, and no one will rescue them. [32]Your sons and daughters will be given to another nation, and you will wear out your eyes watching for them day after day, powerless to lift a hand. [33]A people that you do not know will eat what your land and labor

produce, and you will have nothing but cruel oppression all your days. ³⁴The sights you see will drive you mad. ³⁵The LORD will afflict your knees and legs with painful boils that cannot be cured, spreading from the soles of your feet to the top of your head.

³⁶The LORD will drive you and the king you set over you to a nation unknown to you or your fathers. There you will worship other gods, gods of wood and stone. ³⁷You will become a thing of horror and an object of scorn and ridicule to all the nations where the LORD will drive you.

³⁸You will sow much seed in the field but you will harvest little, because locusts will devour it. ³⁹You will plant vineyards and cultivate them but you will not drink the wine or gather the grapes, because worms will eat them. ⁴⁰You will have olive trees throughout your country but you will not use the oil, because the olives will drop off. ⁴¹You will have sons and daughters but you will not keep them, because they will go into captivity. ⁴²Swarms of locusts will take over all your trees and the crops of your land.

⁴³The alien who lives among you will rise above you higher and higher, but you will sink lower and lower. ⁴⁴He will lend to you, but you will not lend to him. He will be the head, but you will be the tail.

⁴⁵All these curses will come upon you. They will pursue you and overtake you until you are destroyed, because you did not obey the LORD your God and observe the commands and decrees he gave you. ⁴⁶They will be a sign and a wonder to you and your descendants forever. ⁴⁷Because you did not serve the LORD your God joyfully and gladly in the time of prosperity, ⁴⁸therefore in hunger and thirst, in nakedness and dire poverty, you will serve the enemies the LORD sends against you. He will put an iron yoke on your neck until he has destroyed you.

⁴⁹The LORD will bring a nation against you from far away, from the ends of the earth, like an eagle swooping down, a nation whose language you will not understand, ⁵⁰a fierce-looking nation without respect for the old or pity for the young. ⁵¹They will devour the young of your livestock and the crops of your land until you are destroyed. They will leave you no grain, new wine or oil, nor any calves of your herds or lambs of your flocks until you are ruined. ⁵²They will lay siege to all the cities throughout your land until the high fortified walls in which you trust fall down. They will besiege all the cities throughout the land the LORD your God is giving you.

⁵³Because of the suffering that your enemy will inflict on you during the siege, you will eat the fruit of the womb, the flesh of the sons and daughters the LORD your God has given you. ⁵⁴Even the most gentle and sensitive man among you will have no compassion on his own brother or the wife he loves or his surviving children, ⁵⁵and he will not give to one of them any of the flesh of his children that he is eating. It will be all he has left because of the suffering your enemy will inflict on you during the siege of all your cities. ⁵⁶The most gentle and sensitive woman among you—so sensitive and gentle that she would not venture to touch the ground with the sole of her foot—will begrudge the husband she loves and her own son or daughter ⁵⁷the afterbirth from her womb and the children she bears. For she intends to eat them secretly during the siege and in the distress that your enemy will inflict on you in your cities.

⁵⁸If you do not carefully follow all the words of this law, which are written in this book, and do not revere this glorious and awesome name—the LORD your God—⁵⁹the LORD will send fearful plagues on you and your descendants, harsh and prolonged disasters, and severe and lingering illnesses. ⁶⁰He will bring upon you all the diseases of Egypt that you dreaded, and they will cling to you. ⁶¹The LORD will also bring on you every kind of sickness and disaster not

recorded in this Book of the Law, until you are destroyed. [62]You who were as numerous as the stars in the sky will be left but few in number, because you did not obey the LORD your God. [63]Just as it pleased the LORD to make you prosper and increase in number, so it will please him to ruin and destroy you. You will be uprooted from the land you are entering to possess.

[64]Then the LORD will scatter you among all nations, from one end of the earth to the other. There you will worship other gods—gods of wood and stone, which neither you nor your fathers have known. [65]Among those nations you will find no repose, no resting place for the sole of your foot. There the LORD will give you an anxious mind, eyes weary with longing, and a despairing heart. [66]You will live in constant suspense, filled with dread both night and day, never sure of your life. [67]In the morning you will say, "If only it were evening!" and in the evening, "If only it were morning!"—because of the terror that will fill your hearts and the sights that your eyes will see. [68]The LORD will send you back in ships to Egypt on a journey I said you should never make again. There you will offer yourselves for sale to your enemies as male and female slaves, but no one will buy you."

Read that again and again. God's promises are sure. They cannot be taken away. Your life's enjoyment and richness will be directly related to your obedience to His commands. And your life, relationships, and health will reflect your love for His commands and your faithfulness to His Word. Let nobody dissuade you otherwise. And teach them to your children as well.

There is nothing old-fashioned about these commands. You have likely memorized them in your schooling. Take them to heart and plant them in your mind. Walk every day with them in the forefront of your thinking. Be on guard against the one who will gladly see you fall away. Be prepared to encounter them when the temptations of life seem too enticing. Arm yourself with the strength that God has given you to resist sin. God will not allow you to be tempted for more than you can resist. Hold fast to these commands and your life will be solid, firm, and sure.

Adhering to these commands takes courage and initiative. Don't be distracted by wayward friends or business colleagues. Don't feel you have to go with the crowd. If the crowd is moving you to betray those very commands that God has laid out for you, and those values taught to you by your parents and grandparents, then you are being called to find a different crowd and stay the course that God has prepared for you.

Never in our lives were we ever betrayed or disappointed for following God's ways. Time and time again, we experienced the joys and peace that attached to honoring His will and commands. Many times those joys were not immediately realized or visible. Sometimes it took a bit of time before we realized what had happened. God rewarded us much later, and only then did we realize it was our reward for standing strong in the face of adversity.

> **My son, do not forget my teaching, but keep my commands in your heart, for they will prolong your life many years and bring you prosperity. (Proverbs 3:1-2)**

CHAPTER 9

Fear the Lord

My son, if you accept my words and store up my commands within you, turning your ear to wisdom and applying your heart to understanding, and if you call out for insight and cry aloud for understanding, and if you look for it as for silver and search for it as hidden treasure, then you will understand the fear of the Lord and find the knowledge of God. (Proverbs 2:1–5)

The Bible is filled with references to fear. We will address two forms of fear. First is the fear that refers to the trust, respect, and honor to be rendered to the Lord. The other fear refers to that character trait or flaw found in humankind around the world. That fear is associated with lack of security, or the personal feelings when disaster is imminent. Our purpose in this chapter is to firstly look at that fear associated with the former, being the trust in, respect for, and honor of the Lord. Then we will talk about trusting in the Lord to overcome the fear related to the human character deficiency.

Do not let your heart envy sinners, but always be zealous for the fear of the Lord. There is surely a future hope for you, and your hope will not be cut off. (Proverbs 23:17–18)

He who conceals his sins does not prosper, but whoever confesses and renounces them finds mercy. Blessed is the man who always fears the Lord, but he who hardens his heart falls into trouble. (Proverbs 28:13–14)

When written communications translate from one language to another, the receiving language transcription does not always carry the same, let alone exact, meaning of the original. While the Lord is an all-powerful being, in no way does He desire to have His precious creatures fear Him as a dreaded monster or ogre. Quite the contrary. God desires that we love Him faithfully and that we be so closely aligned with Him that there be no thought of any other support in our life. The *fear* term used here is more akin to a super-abiding trust and dependence. None can provide anything like the support and protection that the Lord provides, so don't even think of finding another god, person, job, or possession in which to put your trust. As the third chapter of Proverbs says so perfectly:

> **Trust in the Lord with all your heart and lean not on your own understanding; in all your ways acknowledge him, and he will make your paths straight. (Proverbs 3:5-6)**

So many new and wonderful undertakings fill our lives. Yet, we must never forget that resting on our knowledge and wisdom is folly. The Lord knows your every need. He developed a plan for you, and He knows your every reward. Yet, our selfish and sinful leanings far too often take over and we seek to chart our own course. Repeatedly, the pursuit leads to utter failure and disaster.

> **The fear of the Lord is a fountain of life, turning a man from the snares of death. (Proverbs 14:27)**
>
> **Through love and faithfulness sin is atoned for; through the fear of the Lord a man avoids evil. (Proverbs 16:6)**
>
> **Better a little with the fear of the Lord than great wealth with turmoil. (Proverbs 15:16)**
>
> **The fear of the Lord teaches a man wisdom, and humility comes before honor. (Proverbs 15:33)**
>
> **The name of the Lord is a strong power; the righteous run to it and are safe. (Proverbs 18:10)**

I, wisdom, dwell together with prudence; I possess knowledge and discretion. To fear the Lord is to hate evil; I hate pride and arrogance, evil behavior and perverse speech. (Proverbs 8:12–13)

The fear of the Lord adds length to life, but the years of the wicked are cut short.(Proverbs 10:27)

A wise man fears the Lord and shuns evil, but a fool is hotheaded and reckless. (Proverbs 14:16)

The righteous man is rescued from trouble, and it comes on the wicked instead. (Proverbs 11:8)

Be sure of this: The wicked will not go unpunished, but those who are righteous will go free. (Proverbs 11:21)

Whoever loves discipline loves knowledge, but he who hates correction is stupid. (Proverbs 12:1)

He who listens to a life-giving rebuke will be at home among the wise. He who ignores discipline despises himself, but whoever heeds correction gains understanding. (Proverbs 15:31–32)

Humility and the fear of the Lord bring wealth and honor and life. (Proverbs 22:4)

Do not be wise in your own eyes; fear the Lord and shun evil. This will bring health to your body and nourishment to your bones. (Proverbs 3:7–8)

From time immemorial, fear of the Lord has been seen as essential to enjoying life to its fullest. The Lord established the ground rules in Exodus when He gave His promise to the children of Israel concerning full obedience and commitment to His commands. Very clearly and succinctly, He commanded that the Israelites heed His commands and precepts. If they would do that, their life would be rewarding and prosperous. They would enjoy the land they were about to occupy and reap the rewards that God was prepared to lay before them.

[1]Sing joyfully to the LORD, you righteous;
it is fitting for the upright to praise him.
[2]Praise the LORD with the harp;
make music to him on the ten-stringed lyre.
[3]Sing to him a new song;
play skillfully, and shout for joy.
[4]For the word of the LORD is right and true;
he is faithful in all he does.
[5]The LORD loves righteousness and justice;
the earth is full of his unfailing love.
[6]By the word of the LORD the heavens were made,
their starry host by the breath of his mouth.
[7]He gathers the waters of the sea into jars;
he puts the deep into storehouses.
[8]Let all the earth fear the LORD;
let all the people of the world revere him.
[9]For he spoke, and it came to be;
he commanded, and it stood firm.
[10]The LORD foils the plans of the nations;
he thwarts the purposes of the peoples.
[11]But the plans of the LORD stand firm forever,
the purposes of his heart through all generations.
[12]Blessed is the nation whose God is the LORD,
the people he chose for his inheritance.
[13]From heaven the LORD looks down
and sees all mankind;
[14]from his dwelling place he watches
all who live on earth—
[15]he who forms the hearts of all,
who considers everything they do.
[16]No king is saved by the size of his army;
no warrior escapes by his great strength.
[17]A horse is a vain hope for deliverance;
despite all its great strength it cannot save.
[18]But the eyes of the LORD are on those who fear him,

on those whose hope is in his unfailing love,
   ¹⁹to deliver them from death
and keep them alive in famine.
   ²⁰We wait in hope for the LORD;
he is our help and our shield.
   ²¹In him our hearts rejoice,
for we trust in his holy name.
   ²²May your unfailing love be with us, LORD,
even as we put our hope in you.—**Psalm 33**

   ¹I will extol the LORD at all times;
his praise will always be on my lips.
   ²I will glory in the LORD;
let the afflicted hear and rejoice.
   ³Glorify the LORD with me;
let us exalt his name together.
   ⁴I sought the LORD, and he answered me;
he delivered me from all my fears.
   ⁵Those who look to him are radiant;
their faces are never covered with shame.
   ⁶This poor man called, and the LORD heard him;
he saved him out of all his troubles.
   ⁷The angel of the LORD encamps around those who fear
him,
and he delivers them.
   ⁸Taste and see that the LORD is good;
blessed is the one who takes refuge in him.
   ⁹Fear the LORD, you his holy people,
for those who fear him lack nothing.
   ¹⁰The lions may grow weak and hungry,
but those who seek the LORD lack no good thing.
   ¹¹Come, my children, listen to me;
I will teach you the fear of the LORD.
   ¹²Whoever of you loves life
and desires to see many good days,
   ¹³keep your tongue from evil
and your lips from telling lies.
   ¹⁴Turn from evil and do good;

seek peace and pursue it.
¹⁵The eyes of the LORD are on the righteous,
and his ears are attentive to their cry;
¹⁶but the face of the LORD is against those who do evil,
to blot out their name from the earth.
¹⁷The righteous cry out, and the LORD hears them;
he delivers them from all their troubles.
¹⁸The LORD is close to the brokenhearted
and saves those who are crushed in spirit.
¹⁹The righteous person may have many troubles,
but the LORD delivers him from them all;
²⁰he protects all his bones,
not one of them will be broken.
²¹Evil will slay the wicked;
the foes of the righteous will be condemned.
²²The LORD will rescue his servants;
no one who takes refuge in him will be condemned.–**Psalm 34**

For a moment let us turn to the human trait of fear. At an early age, children fear the strange and unknown. An unfamiliar person or different surrounding evokes crying and anguish. On through the years a person begins to fear the prospect of failure, pain, hurt or disappointment. Elderly folks fear the prospect of being left alone in the world or being incapacitated with no one to help. God has always been there in those moments of doubt and emptiness. Just look in the Concordance of your Bibles and see how often references are made to "fear" and the need to trust in the Lord.

> **So do not fear, for I am with you; do not be dismayed, for I am your God. I will strengthen you and help you; I will uphold you with my righteous hand. (Isaiah 41:10)**

> **Even though I walk through the valley of the shadow of death, I will fear no evil, for you are with me; your rod and your staff, they will comfort me. (Psalm 23:4)**

In righteousness you will be established; tyranny will be far from you; you will have nothing to fear. Terror will be far removed; it will not come near you. (Isaiah 54:14)

It pains us to think of it, but unfortunately our dear children, grandchildren, and those that follow will experience many moments of fear and desperation. You will anguish over jobs, children, security, friends, or whatever. But God has stated with absolute certainty that those who faithfully trust in Him and obey His commands will have nothing to fear. The Lord will put His shield of protection around His own and keep them from mortal danger. But the condition is to fully and without hesitation or doubt to fully trust His ability to keep your safe in His loving care.

Read the story of Gideon in the Book of Judges or that of Joshua when he prepared to conquer the city of Jericho. God assured them that He was with them and they had nothing to fear. His might and faithfulness was there to assure that those who trusted Him would prevail against all odds.

We implore you our children and grandchildren to be strong and take courage. Know in your hearts that God is there to see that you will overcome. He has plans for you and He will not let the evil forces of the world overcome you.

Be strong and courageous. Do not be afraid or terrified because of them, for the Lord your God goes with you; he will never leave you nor forsake you. (Deuteronomy 31:6)

When those times of fear and anguish begin to take hold in your hearts, kneel down and seek the Lord in prayer. Call on Him to give you the courage and strength to prevail and overcome. Take His power and strength into every battle and see the miraculous works which He can perform. He will never fail you nor forsake you.

CHAPTER 10

Sabbath

Remember the Sabbath day by keeping it holy. Six days you shall labor and do all your work, but the seventh day is a Sabbath to the Lord your God. On it you shall not do any work, neither you, nor your son or daughter, nor your manservant or maidservant, nor your animals, nor the alien within your gates. For in six days the Lord made the heavens and the earth, the sea, and all that is in them, but he rested on the seventh day. Therefore the Lord blessed the Sabbath day and made it holy. (Exodus 20:8–11)

Quite simple, isn't it? Quite easy to understand! Can't get it too wrong, one would think. But oh, how we have done exactly that (gotten it wrong, that is) over the years and ages. The Sabbath has ever so slowly, but surely, lost its God-mandated command to rest. We have recast it into another holiday to gratify man-centered rituals. With almost every human pastime activity scheduled for Sunday, and with a host of personal and work functions scheduled for the Sabbath, worship has become too much to bear—we can hardly slip it in between football, baseball, NASCAR, and soccer games, not to mention picnics and water sport activities. Rest and meditation is probably the farthest thing from our thoughts.

But most disconcerting is that we have now gotten to the point where even far too many ministers of the Word and elders of the church have lost the ability to articulate what is, or is not, acceptable Sabbath observance. Most ministers and church leaders have succumbed to the accepted practice of leaving the "right" Sabbath observance to the interpretation of each practicing Christian. To promulgate a list of rules of dos and don'ts would be far too autocratic and much too risky, and possibly smash every toe in the place. We certainly can't have any absolutes in the church since one never knows who will take offense, set off in a fit of anger, and leave the church. And with ever declining church attendance across the country, we sure don't want to see any more irritated Christians—especially the paying ones!

The temptations and pressures of life today seem ever so enticing, enchanting, and all consuming. We find that every relaxation activity known to mankind has worked its way into a time slot on Sundays. Mondays or Tuesdays just never seem to have the same appeal as a Sunday. The daily grind has become overwhelming and there's a need to get away for the weekend, or unwind, or be reconnected and get away from it all.

It is no accident that the Lord references a faithful observance of the Sabbath no less than thirteen times in the book of Exodus. Have any idea what happened to "the man" mentioned in Numbers 15:32–36? It's an interesting and fascinating little story, and yet powerful enough to make you stand up and take notice. Sandwiched within the main text is this little vignette about a certain man in Israel who engaged in what he thought was an obvious, minor little household chore. When he went out and collected wood on the Sabbath, he defied a very clear and concise admonition to remember the Sabbath day to keep it holy. Well, what happened? You've probably guessed it—he was stoned to death. That was after the Lord made it clear to Moses what should be done. Wow. Pretty intense, and this for picking up a little supply of wood on the Sabbath. Was such a drastic reaction necessary? The Lord made it clear to all mankind when He said in Deuteronomy 5:

> **Observe the Sabbath day by keeping it holy, as the Lord your God has commanded you. Six days you shall labor and do all your work, but the seventh day is a Sabbath to the Lord your God. On it you shall not do any work, neither you, nor your son and daughter, nor your manservant or maidservant, nor your ox, your donkey or any of your animals, nor the alien within your gates, so that your manservant and maidservant may rest, as you do. Remember that you were slaves in Egypt and that the Lord your God brought you out of there with a mighty hand and an outstretched arm. Therefore the Lord**

your God has commanded you to observe the Sabbath day. (Deuteronomy 5:12–15)

Then in Isaiah, we read:

If you keep your feet from breaking the Sabbath and from doing as you please on my holy day, if you call the Sabbath a delight and the Lord's holy day honorable, and if you honor it by not going your own way and not doing as you please or speaking idle words, then you will find your joy in the Lord, and I will cause you to ride on the heights of the land and to feast on the inheritance of your father Jacob. The mouth of the Lord has spoken. (Isaiah 58:13–14)

As we said earlier, Sabbath observance has eroded so badly during the centuries that far too many of today's pastors and Christian leaders are unable to articulate its place in our daily lives, let alone articulate a standard we can and should live by. Every Christian is called upon to define his or her definition. In so doing, we gravitate to the lowest common denominator in Sabbath observance.

During the time of Christ, the Jewish leadership had restrictively defined the dos and don'ts of Sabbath worship. Spiritual leaders had totally obliterated the true purpose of the Sabbath—that being a day of rest—a day of worship and reconnection with our Lord. God set out to make this a day of rest and refreshment for man, knowing the human need for physical, mental, and spiritual refreshment and renewal. That meant the day was to be exactly that, a day to rest, refreshment, and worship. But excessive preoccupation with personal enrichment or gratification led the Israelites then, as well as us today, to carry the "rest" thing to excess. Suddenly, we find our rest pursuit so controlling and all consuming that eventually worship is disregarded, rest is never achieved, and refreshment is left to the next weekend.

We found during our own personal growing in the Spirit that faithful observance of the Sabbath was always essential and foundational to our faith and in setting out on our weekly schedule. The Lord always gave us the time to get our work, our hobbies, our recreation, and our personal pursuits accomplished in six days. Sunday was a day of personal rest, refreshment, and worship. Oh, sure, we erred at times and did not always faithfully follow this observance. But having kept our minds focused on the true purpose of the Sabbath, we found that the Lord abundantly and richly blessed our work endeavors and enabled us to experience the rich, tangible blessings that attach to faithful observance of His commands given so repeatedly in the Bible.

Faithful Sabbath observance is especially challenging, owing to the social pressures from friends, family, work associates, and even fellow Christians. Faithful observance seemed especially difficult in our younger years. Social practices often pressured us to believe that a day of rest or a day of refreshment was for older folks. Don't believe it! God never made a qualification of Sabbath observance based on age. Learning to practice faithful observance early on makes it much easier to be faithful in later years. Seldom in our lives did we see friends or neighbors get to an older age and suddenly begin to practice a more faithful Sabbath observance. Quite the opposite was the rule. If it didn't start at an early age, it didn't get any better, it usually got worse!

Train a child in the way he should go, and when he is old he will not turn from it. (Proverbs 22:6)

Throughout the Bible, the Lord continues to admonish His people to observe the Sabbath faithfully. That admonishment is made because the natural tendency of the human race is to use the Sabbath for its own worldly pursuits. God wanted us, as He wants you now, to enjoy the Sabbath as a day of refreshment and renewal; to get your lives in order, and to reconnect with Him in a loving and joyous way that only physical rest can do.

If you seem to be struggling with a job, or with a family trial, or with a troubled feeling, do an honest reality check on your Sabbath observance. The Lord makes a very clear connection between your daily life habits and the rewards available. Sabbath observance is important to the Lord. He made the day and He set the rules for observance. Those who choose to write their own rules are barking up the wrong tree. Tread at your own risk; it's not proclaimed as frequently as it should be, but know that God has a magnificent reward for you if you choose His very simple, yet challenging to implement, plan for your life. *Carefully follow His precepts and a life of fulfillment awaits you.* Sabbath observance should be right up there at the top of the list. Try it. It works. It did for us and it will for you.

We have seen the progression:
- complacent Sabbath observance leads to
- complacent church attendance, which leads to
- complacent study of God's Word, which leads to
- less association with fellow believers. Travel the world and see.

So you ask, "What do I do on a Sunday?" Here's a good start. Sabbath activities might (the first two are a must) include:

- Church attendance
- Bible reading and intensive study
- Literature reading
- Walking
- Personal study and knowledge enrichment
- Time to view the garden, not till it

Vacations also seem to have become an escape from church attendance. Americans, as well as most every other nationality, treasure their vacation (holiday) times. The rapid pace of business and family life today make vacations even more essential. We use vacations as a time to renew and unwind, a time to recharge the batteries, and a time to reconnect with family. A two-week or three-week vacation can quickly become a burden given the higher expectations of vacation experiences. Vacations just aren't what they use to be. A trip to the nearest big city is no longer considered a vacation. Nor is a trip to nearby lakes and streams. Today, we have to jet off to far-flung reaches of the country or the globe. Just getting to and from some of these spots is a backbreaking challenge. Establishing yourselves and seeing the sights is essential. After all, who would pay for such an expensive vacation and not see and experience the sights and catch the favorite tourist attractions?

So now, after this, how does Sunday worship attendance play in your schedule of events? Surely, we aren't taking a vacation from that as well. After all, God's commands state that the Sabbath is a break from the work of six days. Have we begun to get this backward and believe that the vacation (the break from the work of six days) is a break from the Sabbath worship? Surely, God has not said so. Take the Lord with you on your vacation and make the Sabbath a time to worship Him. Use the distant location as a time to reconnect, albeit from a different geographical landmark. Worship Him always wherever you go.

Consider it a privilege that you can worship the Lord in freedom and without fear or threat. There are churches on nearly every street corner and each church is God's way of calling to you. Some may not be to your particular taste or liking, but for sure, there are churches to your liking. Take care you do not shun the Lord's calling by making unfair value judgments about a particular church or denomination. In the next chapter, we talk about church attendance.

Observing the Sabbath is a command to you, just as it was to countless generations before us. Listen to God's calling, His command, and His promises. Sabbath worship is essential, it is wholesome, and it is profitable. Practice it faithfully, and you will come to know the joys and richness that accrue to the faithful Sabbath observer.

CHAPTER 11

Church Attendance

One thing I ask of the Lord, that is what I seek: that I may dwell in the house of the Lord all the days of my life, to gaze upon the beauty of the Lord and to seek him in his temple. For in the day of trouble he will keep me safe in his dwelling; he will hide me in the shelter of his tabernacle and set me high upon a rock. (Psalms 27:4–5)

It only seems fitting that church attendance should follow the chapter about the Sabbath. When work began on this publication, we never thought of having to address the issue of church attendance. From our youth, attending church every Sunday was such a part of our lives that we never really gave it a second thought. Two worship services each Sunday was commonplace, along with a Sunday school class. Add to that regular catechism classes during the week for children, and Bible study classes for adults. Participation at church was a very central part of our lives as well as those with whom we associated. The whole community of believers rallied around the church, and the church was the center of worship, community, and social activities.

Sadly, for the broad mass of society, that is not the case today. It is common to live in a neighborhood where you may be the only one going to church on a Sunday morning. A golf match or a breather from the hustle of daily life makes Sunday mornings a weekly vacation break. After all, the neighbors haven't gone to church in years and their life seems to be doing just fine. Anyway, church seems to be so irrelevant in today's fast-paced, complex world. Church just doesn't seem to excite some people.

In today's world, there is every rationalization floating around telling us why we don't have to be a church member, or that we don't have to go into a church building to be a Christian. Two services have given way to one service. Television and the Internet have brought the church into our living rooms. We can listen to a sermon, be entertained with a praise experience, even send off our contributions by credit card, and never interact with a single living human being. It becomes comfortable to be a Christian with this convenience. Some will say this is the way to worship. Also, some will say that they don't have to be confronted by an elder or a deacon about attendance habits, or have to face the pastor and explain why he hasn't seen them in awhile. Then we so easily rationalize that today's churches are filled with so many hypocrites that appear to be no different from the run-of the-mill person on the street.

Well, we need to dispel that myth right at the outset:

- It is absolutely essential to physically attend church and attend regularly.
- It is absolutely necessary to gather with fellow believers to grow in God's Word.
- It is absolutely necessary to gather with fellow believers to gain strength through the feeling of unity while pursuing a common faith.

What has happened to church attendance in the United States, let alone Europe and the rest of the world? During the last two centuries, advancements in science, technology, industry, and education have ever so slowly, but surely, given man the feelings of self-sufficiency, self-dependency, and self-control. Some will say,

"Who needs a God, much less a church, to provide or satisfy my needs?"

"My mind and body needs (read that as *wants)* are totally fulfilled, nurtured, gratified, or satisfied with the material provisions the world has to offer."

"I have no other needs. I have no other dependencies. My job, my investments, my friends, my cars, and my whatever-you-can-name, meets all I'll ever need."

Well, don't believe it for a minute.

During the years, we have seen countless friends, business colleagues, neighbors, community leaders, government officials, and relatives pursue the dream of material gratification, seemingly believing that the total collection of life's toys and things was the road to contentment. What folly.

One after another, they were led down a road of deception only to be deserted, destroyed, ruined, or drained of all life to eventually be driven to senseless despair. Many went down that road and came to the realization that all was empty and hopeless. Those same individuals later came to a most blessed realization that true joy and richness was to be found in the Lord. Oh, to see their faces shine in happiness and appreciation when fellow Christians gathered around them *at church* to embrace them and give them the hope of the Spirit and joy in their new-found faith and contentment.

What did the leaders during Bible times have to say? Look at what the writers of scripture had to say about the value of worship and the regular congregation of believers:

> **Let us not give up meeting together, as some are in the habit of doing, but let us encourage one another—and all the more as you see the Day approaching. (Hebrews 10:25)**

> **But if we walk in the light, as he is in the light, we have fellowship with one another, and the blood of Jesus, his Son, purifies us from all sin. (1 John 1:7)**

You will no doubt have experiences at a church that are less than comfortable, less than inviting, less than friendly. It has always been thus, and unfortunately will be forever. Churches are comprised of human beings with nuances and idiosyncrasies.

The church of Christ stands as the continuum for propagating the Word of God and for building and growing those who have been called to salvation. Churches large and small are crafted to meet the needs of the members and to provide a foundation to nurture those who have come to know the faith and to equip those in the church to reach out to those who do not yet know the faith.

As you read this, perhaps years after this was written, there is a very real likelihood that one, or all of you, will have drifted from the faith or at least have been excessively casual about your church attendance. We have seen that happen so often in our lives. Our hearts cry out for the Holy Spirit to reach out and touch the hearts of you who have drifted away. But not all is lost, not at all. The church is there to reach out when you feel the working of the Holy Spirit in your life. The church stands ready to give you the comfort and support when all friends have failed you.

To make the church the strong and vibrant institution God meant it to be, a place where you are called to play a role, you have to be active in the church. You have to give of yourself in the making of the church and to make it what it was meant to be. Here is where your gifts come in. God has equipped you with gifts and talents to use in the building of His kingdom and in projecting that kingdom throughout this world. No matter what your gift is, it can be used to the glory of God and in the edification of His kingdom.

A church should rightfully provide its members a:

- Haven of rest
- Place of worship
- Quiet time for study
- Fellowship with fellow Christians
- Opportunity for service
- Sharing of gifts
- Support in times of need

We talked earlier about Sabbath observance. This chapter naturally follows that chapter for a reason. Church attendance is the foundation of Sabbath observance.

> **So is it with you. Since you are eager to have spiritual gifts, try to excel in gifts that build up the church. (1 Cor. 14:12)**

So, if you have drifted, get back to church. Find a church that preaches the Word, prays with all intensity, praises God in its worship, administers the sacraments, and a congregation that reads the Bible. Don't wait and don't hesitate. If you've drifted and are now reflecting on your less-than-regular church attendance, you are experiencing the working of the Holy Spirit in your life. The voice of God is calling to you. Heed His call. Attend church every week. Hear the Word preached. Read the Bible and listen to the readings from the Bible. If the Bible isn't read in that church, find a different church. It is a place to experience and worship God. Preaching, teaching, and reading the Word are essential foundations of the church. Without these, a church is nothing more than a weekly club meeting.

CHAPTER 12

Tithing

Bring the whole tithe into the storehouse, that there may be food in my house. "Test me in this," says the Lord Almighty, "and see if I will not throw open the floodgates of heaven and pour out so much blessing that you will not have room enough for it." (Malachi 3:10)

Now we get to a nice meaty and weighty issue—tithing. Take a moment and read that passage above from Malachi several times. We would venture to guess that very, very few people, let alone Christians, are aware of this passage. Certainly, we missed it for the first fifty years of our lives. Tucked away in the third chapter of the last book of the Old Testament among the Minor Prophets does not particularly place the passage in a very prominent position. One would think that something of such great importance, such promise, and of such value would have been written in bold letters on page one of Genesis! But no, here it is from Malachi, well after the Israelites were afforded opportunity after opportunity to experience and to enjoy the riches of everything God had to offer. Human greed and evil continued to sap the hearts of the children of God. After years of captivity, years of hardship, and years of wandering, Israel once again needed to be reminded of a very simple command and with it a very sure promise.

Abiding in the faith meant practicing God's commands. Early in Deuteronomy, God instituted worship and social commands. Throughout Deuteronomy, Moses challenged the people with the blessings that would result from their faithful observance of God's commands, particularly including the act of rendering onto God a tribute of sacrifice.

> **A tithe of everything from the land, whether grain from the soil or fruit from the trees, belongs to the Lord; it is holy to the Lord. (Leviticus 27:30)**

From there on, and time after time, the Israelites squandered the opportunity to enjoy limitless wealth. Finally, after years of captivity under the Assyrians and the Babylonians, God once again showed His promise and faithfulness. He instructed them about the surety of His command to give onto Him His due and thereby give hope to His people. He now prepares them for a return to their land and a return to being His people. God knows that riches and wealth are at the core of every man's evil desires. Those who are willing to give back to God what He so unselfishly gave in abundance are now being put on notice that He will "open the floodgates of heaven" with blessings beyond compare if only they return a portion to Him.

Tithing was an early discipline established by the Lord as the Israelites were asked to demonstrate their heartfelt love and gratitude for all the bountiful blessings given by God to man. Tithing was instituted as a tribute to God as He gave his commands to the new nation of Israel about to enter the promised land. See how Deuteronomy puts it as the Lord, through Moses, gives his last instructions before Moses is taken from earth and Joshua is about to assume command and bring God's people to their promised inheritance:

> **When you have entered the land the Lord your God is giving you as an inheritance and have taken possession of it and settled in it, take some of the first fruits of all that you produce from the soil of the land the Lord your God is giving you and put them in a basket. . . . Place the basket before the Lord your God and bow down before him. And you and the Levites and the aliens among you shall rejoice in all the good things the Lord your God has given to you and your household. (Deuteronomy 26:1–11)**

What a beautiful entreaty and what a simple way to express gratitude to God for His bounty and blessings. *Oh, simple is it!* Then why did we, in our day, and as it will be in your day, seem to have such a hard time getting people, let alone Christians, to understand that tithing is a foundational pillar on which stood our faith?

Tithing is not a tax, it is not a penalty, and it is not even a charitable gift. Tithing is first a command of God. Read that verse again. Tithing is a love expression; an expression of gratitude for all God has brought us through every hour, every day, every week, and every year of our lives. Look at verses 2–11 of that Deuteronomy passage and you will see that the tithe was a thanksgiving to God for all His bountiful goodness and love through every period of trial and adversity.

We all seem to have a problem parting with our worldly possessions and offering them freely at the table of the Lord. In our day, it has been estimated that the *average Christian* gives about 2 percent of his income to charity, including the House of the Lord. Churches struggle under the weight of rising costs and paltry income. Virtually every church manages to get by making ends meet. Little remains to make a meaningful difference on reaching out to the lost in a forceful way, or ministering to the needs of the poor, hungry, destitute, and homeless.

Isn't it interesting that the US government (as well as every other civilized government on the face of the earth) has devised a system whereby everyone who works for a living not only pays his or her rightfully owed taxes, but also pays them immediately as the services are performed! The government accomplishes this by means of the most ingeniously conceived invention known to mankind—the *withholding tax*. The amount you owe the government is paid before you get your paycheck. Or more correctly stated, you never see it in the first place. The government learned long ago that if left to man's devices, collection of taxes on a man's produce of the soil (his labors) would likely be impossible to achieve, since it is not in a man's heart to give up of what he has first gained possession. The government gets the money even before you have a chance to possess it, assuring the government that it gets its rightful due. And rightful due they get right now!

Well, can you imagine the outcry if everyone had withholding from their wages to cover the amount owing to the Lord? Why not? (Actually, this is done in several European countries today, but not so much out of a duty for tithing as it is a social pressure for reasons too deep for discussion here.) Shouldn't the Lord's command stand above that of the government? Well, it doesn't in our secular society and is unlikely to in the near future. Since withholding is not the system of meeting the tithing command, then every man is left to his own heart's desire and direction in honoring and fulfilling this precept. Quite a load of responsibility and so much at stake. Remember the story of Ananias and Sapphira in Acts 5.

> **Now a man named Ananias, together with his wife Sapphira, also sold a piece of property. With his wife's full knowledge he kept back part of the money for himself, but brought the rest and put it at the apostles' feet. Then Peter said, "Ananias, how is it that Satan has so filled your heart that you have lied to the Holy Spirit and have kept for yourself some of the money you received for the land? Didn't it belong to you before it was sold? And after it was sold, wasn't the money at your disposal? What made you think of doing such a thing? You have not lied to men but to God." When Ananias heard this, he fell down and died. (Acts 5:1–5a)**

Reading the passage further, you know that the same fate befell his wife Sapphira a few hours later. This is not to say that holding back from God what is His in the first place will instantaneously cook you on the spot. But do know that you'll never see a blessing when God sees the self-centered greed in your heart and knows your desire to see yourself come first before Him.

I don't know how many times in our lives we have seen the curse brought upon our friends or us for putting our personal well-being before that of God's. The tithe is a small part of our income, and God sees in our tithe our willingness and faithfulness to put our trust in Him to provide our every need. Withholding our tithes will invariably result in a loss (and rather quickly) even greater than the tithe itself. Just watch. You'll see it happen time and time again. Don't ever fall into the trap of believing this is not a serious matter. In the final book of the Old Testament, God is chastising the nation of Israel after the Jews returned from captivity in Persia. Nehemiah returns to Jerusalem to find that the Jews have ignored the practice of tithing and observance of the Sabbath. Malachi then warns and sounds the alert about the deplorable situation and chastens the people to return to God's commands. Look at the clarity of the Lord's admonishment and His sure promise of being there when they return to Him:

"Ever since the time of your forefathers you have turned away from my decrees and have not kept them. Return to me, and I will return to you," says the Lord Almighty. But you ask, "How are we to return?" Will a man rob God? Yet you rob me. But you ask, "How do we rob you?" In tithes and offerings. You are under a curse—the whole nation of you—because you are robbing me. Bring the whole tithe into the storehouse, that there may be food in my house. "Test me in this," says the Lord Almighty, "and see if I will not throw open the floodgates of heaven and pour out so much blessing that you will not have room enough for it." (Malachi 3:7–10)

Wow, what a promise. What a tremendous indictment of the very source of the Jews' tribulations. Well, the same promise is there for you to grab hold of today. The command for tithing is as true today as it was almost twenty-five hundred years ago. Through faith, you will see that God will abundantly bless your efforts and reward you far beyond your dreams. But *you* need to take the first step by demonstrating that you have complete trust in the Lord. Laying at His table the first fruits of your labors is God's way of seeing your abiding love for Him and showing that you have finally put your full faith and trust in His ability and power to provide your every need. After that, you will see blessings far beyond anything you've ever imagined. You will see the floodgates of heaven pour forth, and the Lord will see you are never in want your entire life. Try it, it works!

Honor the Lord with your wealth, with the first fruits of all your crops; then your barns will be filled to overflowing, and your vats will brim over with new wine. (Proverbs 3:9–10)

CHAPTER 13

Broken and Contrite Heart

The Lord is close to the brokenhearted and saves those who are crushed in spirit. (Psalms 34:18)

As life gathers momentum, so too it gathers baggage. While pursuing friendships or chasing a career, interacting with fellow human beings, or serving your church, you are sure to wrong others and wrong God. No matter what your condition in life, no matter what your calling in life, no matter what your education or economic standing, you are going to sin. And you are going to sin badly. You will break many hearts. You will break your mother's heart, you will break your father's heart, and you will break your girlfriend or your boyfriend's heart. You will commit errors of commission as well as errors of omission. There will be times when you feel you cannot do anything right. There will also be those times when you know what is right, and you will know when you have done wrong and betrayed yourself as well as others.

In John Bunyan's *Pilgrim's Progress*, Christian, the protagonist, enters the Slough of Despond early on in the book. He is covered with the slime of life. His remorse is heavy, and he flounders around seeking a way out. Not until he sees a little gate offering a way to eternal life does he climb out of his desperate situation and set himself on a path of service and commitment to the Lord. He sheds the heavy load of guilt and burden and charts his course to that heavenly reward.

A broken heart and a contrite spirit are spoken of so tenderly and compassionately in the Bible. When our first father Adam sinned, he did more than merely cut himself off from the eternal bliss of the Garden of Eden. Adam set in motion an eternal struggle within himself and his offspring of separation from God. Yet, God was ever faithful. God set in motion a plan to return Adam and all mankind to his love and protection.

When King David first committed the sin of adultery, deceit, and then murder, his heart was heavy beyond understanding. His sorrow was great, and he fully knew he had done wrong. He was the king. He knew he had been chosen by God to be the leader of His people. After all, should not the king be the model of Godly ethics and Godly living? But following Nathan's chastisement of the king's error, David acknowledges his sin and confesses that sin when he says to Nathan:

I have sinned against the Lord. (2 Samuel 12:13)

David realized his wrong. He knew in his heart that it was he, and he alone, who had sinned. Then David did something that for ages men have had a difficult time doing. David humbled himself and confessed his sin to the Lord. He was sorrowful and repentant. He turned from his prideful and evil thought and called upon the Lord for forgiveness. So too, when you commit a wrong and realize the act is wrong and against the will and precepts of God, know that God is looking for you to come to Him with a contrite heart and a confessing spirit. You need to realize that only God can remove a heavy burden, and only He can heal. You need to know that only God offers the true healing medicine for your pains.

He heals the brokenhearted and binds up their wounds. (Psalms 147:3)

As much as you strive to do the will of the Lord, as much as you seek to do the right thing, to follow His precepts and to walk the Christian path, you are going to stumble. You are going to commit wrongs. You are going to sin; we certainly did and more than once. As much as both of us sought to follow the ways of the Lord, we slipped off the path and did wrong. We sinned horribly and brought pain to many around us. Your sin is neither new nor unique. Even those reared in the fear of the Lord commit sins. But the core issue is whether we, like David, acknowledge those sins and go to the Lord with a confessing spirit and a contrite heart. Such is the agony of life. Paul, writing in Romans, felt this very same struggle in his heart when he said:

**I do not understand what I do. For what I want to do I do
not do, but what I hate I do. (Romans 7:15)**

You can sense the conflict in Paul's heart as he recognizes the frailty of man's condition and his (just like yours and ours) easy susceptibility to sin. Obviously, we know that Christ has redeemed us from the penalty of sin and has washed us clean to stand before God at Judgment Day. Yet, He is hurt deep inside His heart knowing that the inclination of man is to do that which is contrary to the will of God.

Now knowing this, does man (or Paul, or you, for that matter) give up? No, not at all. Read the next passage and see what Paul finally sees as his only hope.

**As it is, it is no longer I myself who do it, but it is sin living
in me. I know that nothing good lives in me, that is, in my
sinful nature. For I have the desire to do what is good, but
I cannot carry it out. For what I do is not the good I want
to do; no, the evil I do not want to do—this I keep doing.
Now if I do what I do not want to do, it is no longer I who
do it, but it is sin living in me that does it.**

**So I find this law at work: When I want to do good, evil
is right there with me. For in my inner being I delight in
God's law; but I see another law at work in the members
of my body, waging war against the law of my mind and
making me a prisoner of the law of sin at work within my
members. What a wretched man I am! Who will rescue me
from this body of death? Thanks be to God—through Jesus
Christ our Lord! (Romans 7:17–25)**

We, having become Christians, carry a heavy burden. We carry the guilt of knowing we have sinned, of consciously knowing we have done wrong, and knowing we have violated the will of God. You know it in your mind. You feel it in your heart. It does not feel good. It gnaws at us constantly. We are prone to experience sadness and depression knowing the wrongs can never be undone. That is where we find we have a hope and we have a remedy. Christ died for exactly this condition. Knowing we can never overcome the guilt of sin, Christ came and removed that guilt for the last time. We need carry guilt no longer. We need not feel shame or hurt. Christ has already paid the price, and we are free from that load of guilt.

Nevertheless, how you react to this act of freedom and forgiveness sets in motion two possibly diametrically opposite reactions—one of healing and one of perpetual bitterness, one of comfort and one of loneliness, and one of joy and one of sorrow.

The sacrifices of God are a broken spirit; a broken and contrite heart, O God, you will not despise. (Psalms 51:17)

Be merciful to me, O LORD, for I am in distress; my eyes grow weak with sorrow, my soul and my body with grief. My life is consumed by anguish and my years by groaning; my strength fails because of my affliction, and my bones grow weak. Because of all my enemies, I am the utter contempt of my neighbors; I am a dread to my friends—those who see me on the street flee from me. I am forgotten by them as though I were dead; I have become like broken pottery. For I hear the slander of many; there is terror on every side; they conspire against me and plot to take my life. "But I trust in you, O LORD"; I say, "You are my God." My times are in your hands; deliver me from my enemies and from those who pursue me. Let your face shine on your servant; save me in your unfailing love. Let me not be put to shame, O LORD, for I have cried out to you; but let the wicked be put to shame and lie silent in the grave. Let their lying lips be silenced, for with pride and contempt they speak arrogantly against the righteous. (Psalms 31:9–18)

Then I acknowledged my sin to you and did not cover up my iniquity. I said, "I will confess my transgressions to the Lord"—and you forgave the guilt of my sin. (Psalms 32:5)

There will be disappointments in life. There will be hurts. Whether a broken marital relationship, losing a boyfriend or girlfriend, losing a job, not getting a promotion, losing your home, moving to a lonely neighborhood; any of these will bring on feelings of hopelessness, guilt, or despair. There will be the feelings of hurt or possibly embarrassment. You may not be at fault. You may be the innocent victim of a child's errors, or of a spouse's indiscretions. Your family may suffer the embarrassment of a fellow family member's wrongdoing. At times such as these, you may feel there is nowhere to turn. Life looks so empty. All your dreams have gone up in smoke. And the cause is not the fault of someone else; it all started because of your sin and error. The mistakes may be intentional or unintentional. It makes no difference at this point. The error is done and now there is the price to pay.

Note in King David's case that he also had a price to pay. Yes, David had come with a contrite heart to God. He had confessed his sin. God forgave the sin. But there was still the consequence to pay for that sin, and the act of confession did not remove the penalty. So too in your lives. Our sins have consequences and there are prices to pay. That is God's way of hardening and chastening those He loves. That is the way He implants in our minds the penalties that await us if we sin anew. He so loves us that He desires we never commit that or other sins again. We very possibly may, but in the meantime, God lets us know there will be no easy out.

Then there is the matter of the severity of the penalty. The penalties can be and are painful. They can be so hurtful and stinging. They can leave us with a feeling of loneliness and despair. But God will never so chastise you that there will be no recovery. He wants you to learn from your lessons. He wants to remind you that the next time it happens you will receive a penalty again. This is the human condition. What God is saying is that we should depend on Him. God will never let His children sin beyond the point of hopelessness. He will always keep us from going over the precipice.

Know that we serve a loving God. He wants the very best for us. He wants us to know the detestable nature of sin and wants you and me to seek Him out with love and obedience. Never fail to go to Him with a broken heart. Show your contriteness by overcoming the pride that may keep you from asking forgiveness. God will heal and He will forgive.

CHAPTER 14

Patience

A man's wisdom gives him patience; it is to his glory to overlook an offense. (Proverbs 19:11)

As we turn to the subject of patience, I almost feel a major indictment of my own shortcomings. If there is any one thing that Opa suffered from during the years, it was a lack of patience. Repeatedly, I would anguish over the speed with which something would be accomplished, or I would be short tempered if something wasn't achieved in the period I had in mind. Or, I was always anxiously waiting or anticipating the *next* two or three steps before the *first* two or three steps were achieved.

> **Commit your way to the Lord; trust in him and he will do this: He will make your righteousness shine like the dawn, the justice of your cause like the noonday sun. Be still before the Lord and wait patiently for him; do not fret when men succeed in their ways, when they carry out their wicked schemes. (Psalms 37:5-7)**

Then there was the frustration when an endeavor did not occur as had been expected or a task went in a different direction than planned. Oh, the stomach acids generated over such times and the needless extra heartbeats all because one could not control his patience.

In our later years, we now look back and think of the joy of those who had the patience to see things through, those who had the patience to endure through failings and shortcomings, and those who fully knew the power of God's work to see things through for the glory of His plans, not ours.

> **The end of a matter is better than its beginning, and patience is better than pride. (Ecclesiastes 7:8)**

Our patience is tried at different times in our lives. We anxiously await the acceptance to a college. We wait with bated breath to learn if we are going to get a job offer from that must-have job. The purchase of our first home has us on pins and needles waiting in anticipation for acceptance of our mortgage loan application. We anxiously await the birth of our child, hoping the baby is healthy. A job promotion is at hand, and again we wait with bated breath to learn whether we are the successful candidate.

All of the foregoing examples reference matters of earthly pursuit. All are genuine concerns and worthy of thought. Yet, we must guard against letting any of these overcome our minds and bodies to the extent we become so engrossed that our every thought and waking moment is spent in needless worry and anguish over the decision. See what James had to say about patience in the following passage, and reread the story of Job and the immense suffering and loss he endured.

> **Brothers, as an example of patience in the face of suffering, take the prophets who spoke in the name of the Lord. As you know, we consider blessed those who have persevered. You have heard of Job's perseverance and have seen what the Lord finally brought about. The Lord is full of compassion and mercy. (James 5:10–11)**

> **Do not be anxious about anything, but in everything, by prayer and petition, with thanksgiving, present your requests to God. And the peace of God, which transcends all understanding, will guard your hearts and your minds in Jesus Christ. (Philippians 4:6–7)**

Let's take a closer look at that last passage. Let's assume that we have exhibited patience and understanding. Assume that we have turned to the Lord in prayer at the issue at hand. Then assume nothing has happened. It is now when our patience is tried. Real patience is tested when our prayers do not seem to be having any effect, when time after time we see no results. Then is the time we come to know patience. The waiting and anticipation can be gut-wrenching. We can easily lose our cool and question everything about life. But, just as with Job, God has His time and His pace for working out what He knows is right and good for our lives.

My son, do not despise the Lord's discipline and do not resent his rebuke, because the Lord disciplines those he loves, as a father the son he delights in. (Proverbs 3:11–12)

Over the years, Opa would anguish about the opportunity for a new career. Repeatedly, situations would arise and would appear to be the exact situation that was desired. When the job or career opening would disintegrate, after days and weeks of needless anticipation, hope seemed to vanish, and it appeared a failure could never be replaced. Yet, every time, the very must-have opportunity turned out later to be a colossal disaster, and Opa would look back and thank the Lord for having kept himself from making a most wrongful decision.

As we look back, never once did God *not* know what was precisely right for our lives. He knew the plan, but at times it was not what we necessarily thought was the right one. Oh, thank you, Lord, for your wise and glorious ways, your wonders to behold. I thank the Lord for all the things I did not do, for His wondrous ways of influencing the events of human decisions to keep me from what otherwise would have been catastrophic situations.

Wait for the Lord and keep his way. He will exalt you to inherit the land; when the wicked are cut off, you will see it. (Psalms 37:34)

Advancing age has a way of developing our patience. The older we get, we realize that most things in life will unfold in time. Anxious youthfulness is quite common, and older folks can see it so clearly in the younger people who enter the workforce. That anxiousness can be good. An important element of mature development is having the drive and ambition to improve one's self.

> **We do not want you to become lazy, but to imitate those who through faith and patience inherit what has been promised. (Hebrews 6:12)**

Patience and laziness are sometimes easily confused. Never has God suggested that we sit idly by waiting for everything in life to unfold. God has given us the minds, the willpower, and the energy to better ourselves and to rise to the occasion and meet the challenge. Patience comes in when we have exhausted all our efforts, and then must turn to God for His will to unfold and in His time.

Probably the greatest example of patience is exhibited in the planting, or building, of a new church in a new community. Any young aspiring preacher or church planter will tell you that there are countless hours, days, months, and years of agonizing little steps and minor movements. Frustrations abound and at times, it seems as if nothing is gaining a foothold.

> **Preach the Word; be prepared in season and out of season; correct, rebuke and encourage—with great patience and careful instruction. (2 Timothy 4:2)**

Patience and prayer will always win the day, and God's plan will prevail at the time He sees fit.

Patience is needed in almost every aspect of life, whether family, occupation, the church, in school, in your neighborhood, or in your education. Today's world has become very impatient. The entertainment media has portrayed impatient behavior as the natural instinct and response to any condition that does not go our way or happen in our time frame. Blowing up is portrayed as a valued character trait that shows our power, our manliness, and our independence. We get our way, so we think, if we shout loud enough, fast enough, intensely enough, and with enough bravado. Try that technique with a boss or military superior and see how fast you get to experience the unemployment line. Opa was on the receiving end of such outbursts and knew the hurt they inflict.

> **But the fruit of the Spirit is love, joy, peace, patience, kindness, goodness, faithfulness. (Galatians 5:22)**

Therefore, as God's chosen people, holy and dearly loved, clothe yourselves with compassion, kindness, humility, gentleness and patience. (Colossians 3:12)

Through patience a ruler can be persuaded, and a gentle tongue can break a bone. (Proverbs 25:15)

There is more to patience than just the temporal activities of everyday life. Our calling is sure, and we are here as servants in God's kingdom. Our labors and love must be to do what God wills and to seek answers to what it is He has in mind for us. We wait patiently to hear His calling and to listen for His instructions. We wait patiently for that day when God calls us home for our ultimate final reward. For we all should say, as Paul did in his second letter to Timothy:

I have fought the good fight, I have finished the race, I have kept the faith. Now there is in store for me the crown of righteousness, which the Lord, the righteous Judge, will award me on that day—and not only to me, but also to all who have longed for his appearing. (2 Timothy 4:7-8)

CHAPTER 15

God's Call

Brothers, each man, as responsible to God, should remain in the situation God called him to. (1 Corinthians 7:24)

Somewhere and sometime in your life, you will question your existence and your purpose in life. Times of stress, times of disappointment, times of failure, loss of a job, and loss of a loved one usually characterize these times. It is a normal, natural behavior to look introspectively, ask why you are here, and question why you have to exist.

Then you will likely ask what it is that God has in mind for you. What am I to do with my life?

One of our dear friends, Dr. Ben Johnson, and a man with whom your Opa served (and continues to serve as this is written) on the board of directors at Griffith Laboratories in Chicago, wrote several books on discerning God's will. In his book entitled, *To Will God's Will,* Dr. Johnson states:

> *If you will open yourself to the story of Jesus, you will increasingly become aware of the nature of God as one who comes to us. Your exposure to Jesus will enable you to recognize God in the "burning bushes" of your life.*

> *As you continue to look at Jesus' relation to God, you will see that he depended on God for everything. This fact suggests that all of us are dependent on God for life and breath. Without the presence of God, nothing that is could be. God made everything and sustains everything. During every moment of our being we exist because God sustains us.*

S. Maxwell Coder, former dean of education at Moody Bible Institute, had this to say in his book, *God's Will for Your Life*:

> *One of the most practical and inspiring subjects to be found in the Bible is the revelation that God has a plan for every life. When that plan is discovered and followed, it brings greater happiness and success than could be achieved in any other conceivable set of circumstances. This teaching of the Scriptures has an especially strong appeal to Christian young people with life still before them.*

Recognizing God's call is something unique to each individual. It is not unusual that our assessment of God's calling is not addressed until we attain the age of forty or so. We usually begin to assess that calling because of an external factor such as losing our job, frustration with our job, frustration with our vocation, or the natural instinct to assess our purpose in life. The assessment of our calling in life normally begins over a short period and quite normally can entail several years of challenge and reassessment.

Oftentimes, we find it very difficult to sit back and assess our true purpose in life. When times are good, our income is sufficient, we are in a period of no adversity, and we seldom assess our true calling in life. A more thorough reassessment is usually associated with a crisis in our lives and most often is associated with the loss of a job or the utter frustration with life.

Yet, assessing God's call should not be solely related to our vocation or our daily employment. Seeking out God's purpose for our life should be an ongoing assessment that we seek when we turn to God in prayer. It usually takes an adverse event to drive us to a serious God-centered review of what God has truly called us to be.

Over the years, we have seen countless individuals become frustrated with their lives, usually around the age of forty, and many times they believe they should abandon their vocation or the business world and turn to a life of ministry. While such a calling is commendable and honorable, such a decision process is usually founded on an escape mentality and lacks true critical judgment, let alone listening to God in prayer.

Each of us has been given miraculous gifts by God, and while no one person is blessed with a multiplicity of gifts, each has one or two gifts that are unique, special, and exceptional. So, when we are beginning to assess our calling, it is most important to first assess the gifts God has given us. Then we need to be honest and forthright with ourselves and acknowledge that we will listen to God's Spirit and follow His commands. Far too many people will begin the assessment process only to be diverted to their own selfish whims and ambitions and desires. In every case, that will lead to more frustration and diversion down a path from which they may never return.

The first step in assessing God's calling is to turn to God in prayer. Here we mean truly turning to God in prayer, not merely asking for a particular venture or a particular calling, but asking God to put before us the path that He will have us go. Do not be surprised if the answer is not immediate. God will likely test you to be sure your intentions are well meaning and genuine.

Let us talk a moment about where it is you have come from and what it is you may be called to do. Do not be surprised if where you are coming from is precisely what God is calling you to do. Frustration with your present situation is not necessarily a reason to change directions. Ask God in your prayers to illuminate your present situation and instruct you on what it is that is making the current situation so untenable. Changing a vocation is oftentimes not the answer to relieving life's frustrations. Following God's will and calling will most certainly lead to a more satisfying and fruitful life.

Do not feel that a change in calling will be an answer for greater prosperity. Such may not be the case. God's calling may require you to make a greater sacrifice. Paul, in Galatians 1:13–17, spelled out how God had called him to a different way of life. This new life did not entail greater worldly riches or human rewards. No, Paul's rewards came through the gathering of God's chosen ones and the spreading of the Gospel throughout the world. Your calling may take on a sacrifice of financial comfort, status, life's comforts, or physical well-being. So be it! Be prepared to hear that calling and respond to God's will.

None of this is to say that there is not a genuine reason and purpose in making a life-changing experience in your calling. During the years, Opa served in various business capacities, each of which presented a unique opportunity, yet capitalized on the unique financial skills God had given him. So too, Oma demonstrated her God-given gifts through untiring and exceptional service to Christian schools, Christian women's clubs, and other kingdom service institutions. Both Oma and Opa used their gifts in support of activities in their church, whether leading financial capital campaigns, Bible study groups, or organizational activities. Both stood ready to extend their energies and gifts freely in service to the Lord, all the time helping to expand His kingdom.

Let us say a word about the process of seeking God's will. Be discerning and full of wisdom as you seek the advice of others. Friends, family, and business associates can be helpful, but at the same time, they can be harmful. While we will talk shortly about the importance of friends, it is extremely important you seek out wise counsel in the process of learning God's will. While prayer should be the first start, you will also need to seek out counsel from a variety of sources. You may turn to a pastor, you may turn to a fellow business associate, or you may turn to a trusted family friend. But always challenge whether that person understands and appreciates the importance of God's will for your life.

Let us now turn to a discussion of God's calling for your life and other responsibilities you may have in life's arena. You may be married and possibly have children. Your spouse may have a most satisfying, well-paid employment position, and is most satisfied with that position. If you are around the age of forty, you may still have children whom you are supporting, or children in college who require monetary help to finish their education.

Many are the plans in a man's heart, but it is the Lord's purpose that prevails. (Proverbs 19:21)

During your later years, changes in careers or geographical location may present several challenges. You may be frustrated with your job, you may feel there is something more substantive you've been called to do, or you may feel the rat race just isn't worth the sacrifices and pain. But you now have more responsibilities—family, children, parents needing assistance, your community and church responsibilities—not to mention your level of compensation. All are valid considerations and only you can make the decision whether you are prepared to make a change. But be sure that the change is springing from the Lord's calling in your heart. Ask God for discernment and wisdom in testing the inclination of your heart. Once you have taken it to God in prayer, feel confident that God will lead you to make the right decision.

CHAPTER 16

Service

What good is it, my brothers, if a man claims to have faith but no deeds? Can such faith save him? Suppose a brother or sister is without clothes and daily food. If one of you says to him, "Go, I wish you well; keep warm and well fed," but does nothing about his physical needs, what good is it? In the same way, faith by itself, if it is not accompanied by action, is dead. (James 2:14–17)

The Christian life is founded on a firm faith and a commitment to God. The New Testament makes it very clear that salvation comes from believing in the Lord Jesus Christ. Faith, and faith alone, is sufficient. Having a firm faith is the only way to gain eternal life with Christ in glory. That is why we started this book with a chapter on faith. Faith starts it all. Through our faith, we know that the Bible is the inspired Word of God; through faith, we know that God exists and He reigns supreme. We know that through the death and resurrection of Jesus Christ, we have life, and we can look forward to eternity with God the Father and our Lord Jesus.

James added a most magnificent element—in a sense a litmus test—in assessing our faith, a measure to tell whether it is genuine or not. Merely saying we have faith leaves much to be desired. For after all, our words, deeds, thoughts, and actions tell whether that faith has had a real life-changing influence in our hearts. Does our life really and honestly display a faith-based life? Saying we have faith would naturally assume that we have aligned our hearts with Christ and desire to live in His ways and serve in His kingdom. James is saying that our faith will manifest through the way we act, the way we go about working for God's kingdom, and the way we practice these principles in our daily lives. This has been a challenge to the Christian faith and to theologians over the centuries. But James brings the matter to a real life experience. He is saying that if you are not practicing your faith in an action way, then it is very likely that your faith is not what you may think it is!

A life of service does not come naturally to most human beings. Largely, the human spirit (as tempted by the devil), is inclined to seek after those things that selfishly satisfy one's personal interests. While our hearts were originally created to love God our Creator and to love one another, sin polluted that inclination, and we became totally self-centered and debased in our relationship and attitude toward serving God.

Once you have expressed a faith in Christ and committed to a Christ-centered life, a transformation occurs. We feel a wellspring of joy that flows from deep within our soul. Before long, we want to share that joy with as many other fellow human beings as possible. We earnestly desire to reach out and be of help (service) to all who will receive our assistance.

Service takes many forms. Looking at our talents and the skills God has given us is a great place to start. As we look at you children, we see talents of amazing quality. The gifts you have been given are already beginning to show in your expression of interests. As grandparents, we have seen the unfolding of your special talents and the natural inclinations you have for particular endeavors, whether in the area of the arts, sports, science, nature, business, or whatever.

The end of all things is near. Therefore be clear minded and self-controlled so that you can pray. Above all, love each other deeply, because love covers over a multitude of sins. Offer hospitality to one another without grumbling. Each one should use whatever gift he has received to serve others, faithfully administering God's grace in its various forms. If anyone speaks, he should do it as one speaking the very words of God. If anyone serves, he should do it with the strength God provides, so that in all things God may be praised through Jesus Christ. To him be the glory and the power forever and ever. Amen. (1 Peter 4:7–11)

Cast your bread upon the waters, for after many days you will find it again. (Ecclesiastes 11:1)

Our service must be unselfish and with no desire to gain personal benefit from our undertakings. Giving of your gifts should be a wellspring of love to your community, to your friends, to your coworkers, and to those in need. God has dearly blessed you with indescribable gifts that your willingness to give should never be tainted with a desire to get something out of it. Give unselfishly and you will see untold gifts return to you. Even though the undertaking seems for the moment to yield no results, God will see to it that your work is not in vain. Those results very likely will not mean personal enrichment (in terms of earthly, material riches) to you, they are most likely returns enriching to someone else. Giving from your heart is the secret; God knows your intent, and He knows your every desire and inclination.

You have no doubt heard the phrase "it is more blessed to give than to receive." That is the foundation of a life of service. Don't ask what you will get out of it, but rather ask how much you can give. Give with love and generosity. Your reward will be found in the life hereafter, springing from a faith underpinned by a heart of love, compassion, and caring.

Service can be public or private. Much service will be done anonymously, unseen, and unknown to those around you. That is good and wholesome. Anonymity can assure that you are not inclined to win the glory of your fellow men. For God alone knows what is done in secret. He sees your work, and He alone will reward you for your service. Your reward comes when you have done the will of the Lord and know that you have shared the gifts He has given you. You are showing gratitude to Him through service to others.

So what service can you do? Where do I begin and when? Service is reaching out to those who are in need—the oppressed, the destitute, the poor, the underprivileged, the infirmed, the incarcerated. It is sharing, caring, and healing. There is no end to the needs of the church, the community, the Christian schools, the homeless missions, the institutions of mercy. There are the hopeless, the lonely, the products of broken families, the fatherless, and the motherless. There are the wandering, the destitute, the depressed, and the brokenhearted. They are all around you—in your neighborhood, your workplace, your church, your school, and your family. They are nearby or they are in another part of the country or the world. They are in the hospitals or in the substance abuse centers. Look around and you will see pain, suffering, hopelessness, and despair.

Every institution of mercy is crying out for volunteers, for ministers of mercy, for aides to help with the daily tasks of caring, feeding, counseling, or just being there. Your church offers countless opportunities for reaching out to the homeless, the sick, the depressed, the addicted, the lonely, and the infirm. Incidentally, if your church does not appear to be *actively* involved in reaching out to the poor, the downtrodden, the imprisoned, or the needy, find another church. No church should be so involved with itself as to forget the needs of the less fortunate of society. This is precisely what James is talking about, a faith without works is no faith at all. If our works or actions don't live out in reality what our faith says we should be, we are a hopeless lot, and God will surely not bless our lives or our efforts, even here on earth.

So, you may ask, how much time should I devote to service? How do I balance this service with everything else I do in life? Before you answer that question, look at your weekly or monthly schedule right now. People who are serving sincerely will generally tell you that they need not worry themselves with tallying the hours they devote to service. Rather, you will find that people who are actively engaged in service give of their time generously, willingly, and without counting the hours. Their service is a labor of love and compassion.

You may want to look at it from a different perspective. How much time am I devoting to personal gratification, to personal enrichment, to entertainment, to recreation, and so on? The best way to determine where a person's heart is, is to look at his or her calendar and checkbook. If we looked at your calendar, would it show a generous allotment of time to kingdom service? Would it show an abundance of time devoted to reaching out to the poor, the economically disadvantaged, the sick, the school dropouts, the orphans, and the depressed? Or is your service time devoted to sitting through meaningless meetings, talking about problems but never doing anything about those problems? Do you, and those you may be serving with, talk about the poor, analyze the poor's plight, but never actually meet the poor?

Service is also a wonderful way to engage with other fellow believers of similar persuasion. Whether with your spouse, your closest business associate, or your church's ministry leaders, you can be even more effective when two or more undertake a service activity. Latch on to those who share a similar passion for your particular ministry interest. Grow together in the spirit of giving. Walk with someone who is more interested in giving than receiving. From this, you will begin to experience the true joy of Christian unity and the richness that comes from using your gifts in the advancement of the kingdom.

CHAPTER 17

Balancing Life

So I hated life, because the work that is done under the sun was grievous to me. All of it is meaningless, a chasing after the wind. I hated all the things I had toiled for under the sun, because I must leave them to the one who comes after me. And who knows whether he will be a wise man or a fool? Yet he will have control over all the work into which I have poured my effort and skill under the sun. This too is meaningless. So my heart began to despair over all my toilsome labor under the sun. For a man may do his work with wisdom, knowledge and skill, and then he must leave all he owns to someone who has not worked for it. This too is meaningless and a great misfortune. What does a man get for all the toil and anxious striving with which he labors under the sun? All his days his work is pain and grief; even at night his mind does not rest. This too is meaningless.

A man can do nothing better than to eat and drink and find satisfaction in his work. This too, I see, is from the hand of God, for without him, who can eat or find enjoyment? To the man who pleases him, God gives wisdom, knowledge and happiness, but to the sinner he gives the task of gathering and storing up wealth to hand it over to the one who pleases God. This too is meaningless, a chasing after the wind. (Ecclesiastes 2:17–26)

Life at times feels like a runaway freight train. There seems no end to the demands on our time. The modern world sets more and more demands and more and more priorities for our lives. There hardly seems enough time in a day or in a week, or in a year, to attend to all the matters of life.

As if just plain living is not enough, our work, our community, our church, and our friends seem ever more demanding. Just in an average community, there is no end to the number of worthwhile organizations where one can contribute time and talent. Today's more complex business world makes for a more time-consuming and time-demanding environment. The dynamics of a world economy make for a far more stressful and time-consuming career environment than it did fifty or one hundred years ago. With the advent of electronic communications, the Internet, voice mail, and instant messaging, we live in a world that demands instant attention and instant response to whatever issue is at hand.

Then there is the social stigma attached with being a workaholic. On one hand, we are charged with being a good worker and not being lazy. Hard work is good and wholesome. Yet hard work carried to an extreme can and will become a burden on your life and a cancer on your soul. Some people just do not seem able to extricate themselves from the daily tasks of their vocation. Believe it, there are never enough hours in the day to get everything done.

Greater education, knowledge, and skill bring with it a greater calling and demand for your talents in other arenas of life: church, community, government, etc. After all, did not God give us the talents to use? Moreover, He said to hide not our light under a bushel. Aren't we to use our talents fully in advancing His kingdom? How do we do it all? How do we meet all the needs that seem to be awaiting our calling?

These are important questions, and the answers are not easy. The solutions can be fleeting. Add to this every person's energy level and capacity to process multiple tasks simultaneously and the solution becomes even more evasive. When is too much, too much? Am I too busy with the right things? Where should I concentrate my talents and my time? Am I wearing myself out on the wrong things? Am I wearing myself out on the right things?

First, we need to tell you that this very issue plagued us for many years during our lives. We became excessively busy with a myriad of undertakings in the church, in the community, in the schools, in our occupation, and in our family life. So, the observations you will read about are based on real life experience. We will try to help you avoid some of the mistakes we made. Though you are likely to make many of those we made, be on your guard, and watch for signs of getting out of balance.

We will say right up front that busyness can be healthy. Everybody and every mind is different, and every person possesses a different level of energy to engage multiple tasks simultaneously. Busyness can be detrimental as well. You need to know your capacity to handle tasks. Are the tasks you are trying to undertake fitting into your knowledge arena? Nothing can be more frustrating than to be given an assigned task that is totally outside your skill area or your area of passion.

How you are busy is more the issue than what you are busy with! And, what we are busy with is as important as how much we are busy. Ask yourself a few questions:

- Has my busyness kept me from Sabbath worship? Is it just too much to get out on the Sabbath morning to worship, or is it easier to justify a day to read the paper or watch a little television?
- Has my busyness kept me from faithfully reading the Bible? Are you up to speed with the Bible's teachings? When is the last time you read Haggai? How about Nahum? Do you know their themes and lessons?
- When was the last time you were so busy with football practices that you didn't have time to study the Bible?
- Do you spend every Saturday night on entertainment or on Sabbath preparation?
- Does an inventory of your personal calendar hours show an imbalance of hours devoted to personal pursuits, or to the job? Take a tally during a three-month period and assign hours to family, entertainment, subsistence (sleeping, eating, etc.), occupation, and worship!
- Is your inventory of golf scorecards larger than your inventory of Bible study notes?

Ask yourself what it is that you wish to leave as a legacy to your children and grandchildren. Time is so precious and can never be recovered. Only in later years do we begin to understand the extent of our wasted opportunities and our wastefulness of time. Older people often feel remorse about lost opportunities and wasted years. Most older people remorse not of jobs lost, not of properties or riches unattained, nor of mountains not conquered but of lost time with children, lost time with elderly parents who required a special care need, lost time with fellow Christians, or lost time in serving the less fortunate. For that reason, countless people give unselfishly of their time and talents in retirement for no compensation at all. They know the preciousness of time and the limited amount of time available before God calls them home. We should be thankful to those who so generously give of their time and skills to help in their later years without need for reward or gain.

Yet, while you are young, now is the time to assess the balance of activities in your life. Youthful energy is a blessing, and the ability to multitask is one of those blessings endowed on the young. But in our quest to capture all the good things in life and to experience all the undiscovered wonders of the world, one very soon can become inundated with a multitude of commitments. In very short order, the schedule becomes more a burden than a pleasure.

Here are a few practical thoughts to keep your life in balance:

- Learn to say *no*! Opa had an ongoing challenge—some would say a real problem—in this respect and never really learned to overcome that shortcoming. Oma excelled at this and was a master example of how one should balance time and activities.
- Concentrate your time on what you do best.
- Keep an accurate account of your time every week.
- Never shortchange your worship and prayer time.
- Have time for yourself and your family.
- Read the Bible regularly, every day.
- Make personal time truly personal time—don't mix business with vacations.
- Focus your activities and budget your time for each.

When you seriously begin to chart your weekly, monthly, or yearly goals, make a concerted effort to allocate your time wisely. Make certain that God's work is properly balanced with all other tasks of life. If God's work is under-represented, start a serious challenge of your time and undertakings. Just as with tithes, plan God's work first, then schedule other tasks around other endeavors.

CHAPTER 18

Pressing On

> Not that I have already obtained all this, or have already been made perfect, but I press on to take hold of that for which Christ Jesus took hold of me. Brothers, I do not consider myself yet to have taken hold of it. But one thing I do: Forgetting what is behind and straining toward what is ahead, I press on toward the goal to win the prize for which God has called me heavenward in Christ Jesus. (Philippians 3:12–14)

We have sought to put this publication together without sounding old-fashioned. Yet, now seventy years old, we have gained the ability to give a more insightful perspective on life. Our experiences have enabled us to see with more clarity the values of life than we did in our teens, twenties, or thirties. Our lives experienced many moods, feelings, hurts, desires, broken promises, shattered hopes, and yet joys, love, thrills, excitement, and euphoria.

> Be merciful to me, O God, for men hotly pursue me; all day long they press their attack. My slanderers pursue me all day long; many are attacking me in their pride. When I am afraid, I will trust in you. In God whose word I praise, in God I trust; I will not be afraid. What can mortal man do to me? All day long they twist my words; they are always plotting to harm me. They conspire, they lurk, they watch my steps, eager to take my life. (Psalms 56:1–6)

In the same vein, your lives will be filled with many joys, but also with sorrows and moments of anxiety. There will be those times when all seems so hopeless and lost. You will seem to lose your bearings and life will seem so empty. In our introductory verse above, you can see that Paul sensed those same emotions. He had carried many stripes and burdens for the faith. He had been whipped for the faith and imprisoned. He had been slandered and mocked. He had been falsely accused and stoned. Yet, he understood the importance of pushing forward for the much greater prize. Pressing on for the ultimate goal was ever at the forefront of his mind. Putting behind all the pain and suffering was essential to getting his mind focused on the final prize of eternity with his Lord and Savior.

The Lord has called each of us to fill a need in this world, and He expects us to step up to the challenge and fulfill our Godly responsibility. We have a calling from God, and it is our responsibility to meet the challenge. There will be times when the load and calling seems unbearable and hopeless. You will feel overwhelmed and powerless. But always remember that the Lord will never give us more than we can bear and He says so in His Word.

The psalmist speaks to the emotions you are experiencing when he (King David) says:

> **Then I acknowledged my sin to you and did not cover up my iniquity. I said, "I will confess my transgressions to the Lord"—and you forgave the guilt of my sin. Therefore let everyone who is godly pray to you while you may be found; surely when the mighty waters rise, they will not reach him. You are my hiding place; you will protect me from trouble and surround me with songs of deliverance. (Psalms 32:5–7)**

> **Many are the woes of the wicked, but the Lord's unfailing love surrounds the man who trusts in Him. (Psalms 32:10)**

Throughout our lives, we had those periods when all hope seemed lost, when nothing seemed to go right, when we felt like giving up and fleeing to the wilderness of Alaska, or escaping to some remote island in the Pacific Ocean. At the same time, there was the feeling of embarrassment and humiliation. There's always the feeling that dashed dreams will show that we are actually just like the rest of humanity: simple, forgetful, error-prone, clumsy, and hopelessly careless. Bulletproof we are not. So when that job is not going right, or worse, when it is a heavy burden to go back and face the consequences of a very difficult situation, the Lord cries out, "Press on!"

But it is in not only in our daily work life where the road gets steep and the going gets tough. It happens far more frequently in our family lives, in our relationships with our husband, wife, children, parents, brothers, or sisters. It happens even more painfully in our relationships with our church and with our fellow Christians. Disappointments and frictions abound in the church of Christ and Satan sees a fruitful ground for shaking the faith of saints as he sears the emotions of Christians working to further the kingdom of Jesus Christ. How many times your Opa and Oma experienced this is more than we wish to remember. Whether undertaking Bible study meetings or conducting capital campaigns to expand kingdom worship facilities needed to meet the needs of an ever growing list of brothers and sisters seeking and growing in the Lord, Satan threw his most capable and talented forces to work at dividing the saints gathered together to further the cause.

Cast your cares on the Lord and he will sustain you; he will never let the righteous fall. (Psalms 55:22)

There is not enough space here to tell all the shameful and disgusting means the devil has at his disposal to divide the work of Christians, but suffice it to say, griping and jealousy are the immediate weapons that come to mind when the Lord's work is undertaken. Just see what happens when the design of a new church or a new sanctuary addition is proposed. Try getting five or ten people to agree on the color of the carpet. Try to decide if tradesmen in the church will have preferential treatment in getting the contracts for the painting, masonry, carpentry, cupboards, etc. Or try to get the full commitment of people's money to support the project. Enough said; you begin to get the picture. This is the devil working overtime, because he knows that if he can cause dissension here, then the unchurched will see this and likewise conclude that this is the reason they never wanted anything to do with religion or Christianity in the first place. That sort of success for the devil we need like a hole in the head. Through it all, we need to press on with all conviction and with brotherly love to quest for the banner of Christ and put behind us all the hurt and pain that comes from the divisions that occur among the fellowship of believers.

Pursuing the Lord's work is seldom easy or painless. The way ahead will be tough. It will be lonely. Friends will forsake you. Enemies will take advantage of you. The cost in human economic terms could be high. It may even divide you from other family members. Always remember, God will never permit your spirit to be crushed or your will defeated while pursuing His work. God knows what we have need of and will never forsake us. Just as with temptation, God is there in life's troubling times, as Paul wrote to the Corinthians.

> **No temptation has seized you except what is common to man. And God is faithful; he will not let you be tempted beyond what you can bear. But when you are tempted, he will also provide a way out so that you can stand up under it. (1 Corinthians 10:13)**

Remember this! The reward of eternal life is far richer than anything this world has to offer. Measuring success or failure in God's terms should not be measured on the scales used by the temporal world. Psalm 121 is one of the most inspiring and encouraging passages when you begin to wonder if life is worth it all. The psalmist knew where his support rested and who is there when the going gets rough. Read its words slowly and grasp the spirit of support and strength:

> **I lift up my eyes to the hills—where does my help come from?**
>
> **My help comes from the Lord, the Maker of heaven and earth.**
>
> **He will not let your foot slip—he who watches over you will not slumber;**
>
> **Indeed, he who watches over Israel will neither slumber nor sleep.**

The Lord watches over you—the Lord is your shade at your right hand; the sun will not harm you by day, nor the moon by night.

The Lord will keep you from all harm—he will watch over your life; the Lord will watch over your coming and going both now and forevermore. (Psalms 121)

Read the chapter on prayer and take a moment to ask yourself if you have been taking these cares to God. Ask God for wisdom, not solutions; God will give the solution. Ask God for patience, not timetables. Ask God for strength, not power. If it is God's desire, you will be given the strength and wisdom to prevail and succeed.

We can see examples throughout the Bible of those who pressed on, no matter what the hardships. They pressed on no matter what the world threw at them.

First think of Noah, picked by God because of his faithfulness; Noah found grace in the eyes of the Lord. Following the instructions of God, Noah faithfully persevered in the building of an ark. Can you imagine the ridicule Noah got from the heathens around him? How could there ever be a need for an ark in that barren desert? Yet he persisted and pressed on "and did according to all that the Lord commanded him."

Then look at the example of Joseph. Just imagine the loneliness he must have felt when his own brothers sold him, his own flesh and blood, to a caravan of traders. His mind must have been filled with grief and despair as he traveled that lonely and dusty trail to Egypt. Rest assured, Joseph felt a loneliness we have never experienced, and then to be sold as a slave to Potiphar. Not only that, but to be falsely accused of adultery with Potphar's wife, and then thrown into a prison. Through it all, Joseph persevered, and knew that God was with him and had a plan for him. Then we see how Joseph was raised to a level of authority in Egypt second only to Pharaoh. What a blessing God has when we stand up to adversity and press on for the prize.

Other examples in the New Testament abound, as in the story of Peter when imprisoned by Herod. Then there are the countless experiences of our dear brother Paul and the hardships he endured throughout his missionary journeys.

We should not have to mention, but we will, that you make sure you are pressing on for God-centered initiatives. There will be enough disappointments in life for kingdom-enriching pursuits. Far too often, we can be deceived by letting our pursuit of selfish gains muddy our thinking. Satan is more than pleased to warp our minds, distract our focus, and get us to believe that our personal gain should be first. We can so easily forget where the real goal of life lies and become needlessly frustrated when we don't seem to be getting ahead. At that point, stop and ask yourself if the frustration and failure is related to the pursuit of selfish ambitions. Oftentimes it is. A good recheck can be accomplished by sitting down and quietly taking your anxiety to the Lord in prayer, asking the Lord for wisdom and insight. Ask the Lord to clear your thoughts and manifest His desires to you. Know this, the Lord will never leave you or forsake you. His desire for you will be made known when you take it to Him in prayer.

> **Let us not become weary in doing good, for at the proper time we will reap a harvest if we do not give up. (Galatians 6:9)**

We mentioned earlier that friends, family, business associates, neighbors, and maybe even those in your church or place of worship might betray you. The last group is probably the most painful and the most effective weapon of Satan. Oh, how he relishes the thought of getting the saints to betray the confidences of one another. Just when we thought we had found a place of refuge, there our very hurts are turned on us. The joys we so embraced in the company of fellow believers are rent asunder by the betrayal of a fellow believer. But let us say, in the end, there is no better place to find communion and comfort than in the presence of fellow church members. All are human, and even church members are prone to the evils of pain infliction and hurt. Yet, even with that, there is no organization, group, association, or whatever more supporting than the church. Paul saw this in the church at Corinth. Notice the passage in 1 Corinthians 11:17–18 when he says:

> **In the following directives I have no praise for you, for your meetings do more harm than good. In the first place, I hear**

that when you come together as a church, there are divisions among you, and to some extent I believe it.

So we say to you, our dearly loved grandchildren, and to those after you who are reading this, put your trust in the Lord, cast your cares on Him, press on in the face of adversity, and never give up. Remember, the prize you are questing for stands far above anything the earth has to offer. Your prize awaits you when you join our Lord for a life of eternity with Him and the saints who persevered through the adversities of life.

When the storm has swept by, the wicked are gone, but the righteous stand firm forever. (Proverbs 10:25)

CHAPTER 19

A Loving Marriage

He who finds a wife finds what is good and receives favor from the Lord. (Proverbs 18:22)

For fifty years, Oma and Opa have enjoyed the blessed state of marriage. Next to our relationship with Christ, our marriage has been the most cohesive, supportive, and meaningful relationship during our years on earth. We pray that God will give us even more years to enjoy our fellowship. As we write this, we do not know whether any of our grandchildren will marry. God may call you to remain single. That is understandable and is as fully in concert with God's will as is entering into a marriage. Yet, if you are called to be in a marriage relationship, God has set you in a position of trust and responsibility.

Our years together as husband and wife have been strengthened by our faith in God and joining in seeking out and living His will for our lives. While marriage can be a necessary bond for building that relationship during life, others (and possibly even you) may find that strength and will in an unmarried state.

Marriage is a tremendous responsibility. It is a life-changing event and calls us to understand ourselves better and to learn responsibility and sharing. Starting out in marriage, life is filled with so many new challenges and so many new opportunities. At the same time, conflicts arise and disagreements interrupt the otherwise harmonious relationship. Any relationship between a man and a woman will naturally involve misunderstandings, disagreements, conflicts of interests, and conflicts of time.

Yet, there may come a time in your married life where all seems so hopeless. The joy may seem to evaporate out of the marriage. The disagreements just never seem to stop. You may feel there is no way to find a foundation for understanding and joy. It's at times like this you would do well by taking a look at your spiritual life and ask whether you have truly been faithful in your practice of prayer and in seeking God's will for your life. Have you been taking your cares to the Lord? Have you been faithful in your church attendance? Have you had your life priorities in synchronization with the Lord's will?

There are those events in life that will always test a marriage—discipline of children, money matters, sexual relationships, another person, a difficult work environment, and extended family relatives. There are no doubt more, but if you look at your present situation, it's likely that one or more of those listed here are the root of a strained marriage.

So the question becomes, what do you do about it?

Look back to when you entered your marriage relationship. Remember how joyous and united you were. Remember how you shared common aspirations and visions. Remember how you cherished the moments together: the times during a dinner, the times on a vacation all alone, or the joy of a job promotion. Then there may have been the exciting time experienced upon the arrival of your first child and the euphoria of having brought a life into the world. The first signs of the child talking, walking, and loving are something to behold.

Now the thrill, the joy, the excitement, the richness has somehow evaporated. There just isn't the old zip in the marriage. Happiness seems to be somewhere else—another locality, another person, another job. Marriage abandonment seems a viable option. After all, look at all the other people who have sought the easy way out with divorce; they seem to have found contentment and satisfaction. All looks so rosy and serene. If only I could start over again, I'd do it so differently, you might be thinking.

Well, don't believe that for a moment. Countless millions have found that divorce has usually resulted in jumping from one frying pan into the fire of another. You won't have his or her family issues with your current spouse, but just wait until you see what real family problems are with the new spouse. At least your present husband is willing to work and support a family; see what it's like to have a lazy bum support the family. Don't currently have mother-in-law problems? Just wait, you'll have them in spades with the new mate. The new gal seems so sensuous and enticing, but wait until she is wearing your wedding ring, and then witness how fast the embers cool. Think you had money problems before; see what it is like to support two families when you couldn't make ends meet supporting one! And we haven't even mentioned the cataclysmic emotional damage to children from a broken home. The damage is never repaired, and children will harbor the pain and hurt for the rest of their lives.

While we have seen countless friends, neighbors, and business associates demolish their marriages, we have yet to see even one instance whereby divorce was the answer to happiness. The other person is just not the answer to present marital problems.

So, what does it take to make a marriage work? How can I get my marriage back on track? Where did we go wrong?

First, a beautiful loving relationship in a marriage is found in a beautiful loving relationship with God. Your spiritual life will be a foundation for getting a marriage relationship right and strong. So as we said before, look first at your *prayer life*, at your *church attendance life*, at your *Sabbath observance life*, at your *tithing life*, and at your *Bible study life*.

The writer in Ecclesiastes has a most beautiful thing to say about the value of companionship in marriage:

> **Two are better than one, because they have a good return for their work: if one falls down, his friend can help him up. But pity the man who falls and has no one to help him up! Also, if two lie down together, they will keep warm. But how can one keep warm alone? Though one may be overpowered, two can defend themselves. A cord of three strands is not quickly broken. (Ecclisiastes 4:9–12)**

Then see what Proverbs has to say:

> **A wife of noble character who can find? She is worth far more than rubies. Her husband has full confidence in her and lacks nothing of value. She brings him good, not harm, all the days of her life. (Proverbs 31:10–12)**

> **She speaks with wisdom, and faithful instruction is on her tongue. She watches over the affairs of her household**

and does not eat the bread of idleness. Her children arise and call her blessed; her husband also, and he praises her: many women do noble things, but you surpass them all. Charm is deceptive, and beauty is fleeting; but a woman who fears the Lord is to be praised. Give her the reward she has earned, and let her works bring praise at the city gate. (Proverbs 31:26–31)

Marriage is a most wonderful and beautiful institution given by God to mankind. Through marriage, God provided man and woman with companionship and love. The ability to procreate is embodied in the institution of marriage, and God's blessings are made manifest through the uniting of a man and woman in love.

We are fully aware that not every marriage develops and ends as God would have it to be. Divorce has become most prevalent in our society and current trends do not indicate a slowing. While it is our fondest desire that none of our precious children and grandchildren experience the pain of divorce, we are fully cognizant that such may occur in our family. Of those who are going through, or have gone through, a divorce we pray that the Lord will heal your heart and help you overcome the hurt and disappointment that usually accompanies such a situation. Do know that the Lord is always there to help and heal you. Turn to Him for comfort and solace. The Lord is a comfort in time of need and He will lift you up and carry you to a higher ground. The scars and pain may never quite go away, but do know you have a friend in Christ and His healing is sure and complete.

Your marriage is a bond instituted by Christ and was established for the perpetuation of the faith and humanity. Our Lord sees the relationship between a husband and wife as His own relationship to His church. So care for your marriage . . . work at it . . . nurture it . . . and grow it with the support of Christ and His care. May you find happiness in the marriage relationship to be as fulfilling and joyous as we have. May God bless you richly.

CHAPTER 20

Family

If anyone does not provide for his relatives, and especially for his immediate family, he has denied the faith and is worse than an unbeliever. (1 Timothy 5:8)

A family is one of God's richest blessings and something to be cherished. As you go through life and see the many tragedies and broken hearts experienced by so many people, far too often you can trace the cause back to a troubled family life at an early age. The modern world has ripped the family apart. It has separated husbands and wives, it has separated brothers and sisters, and it has separated parents and children. All the vices at work in the world continue to undermine the strength and bonds of the family. Divorce has run rampant in the world today and has rent children from their fathers, wives from their husbands, and children from their parents. Hardly is a family untouched by the pain and consequences of divorce.

Grandma Schauer raised Opa as an only child, given that his father had died at fifty-two from a fishing accident. She was a woman of exceptional strength and a deeply founded faith. She was one of eleven children (Opa's aunts and uncles), and these individuals became important factors in the raising of Opa. The children of those aunts and uncles (Opa's cousins) became proxy brothers and sisters to Opa and additionally provided a source of strength, nurture, and love. The solidarity of that family provided a rich heritage to model and emulate. Throughout Opa's childhood, all these individuals provided care and lessons that carried throughout Opa's life.

Similarly, Oma was raised in a strong family environment. At an early age, she also was taught the foundations of the Christian faith.

She faithfully attended Sunday school and catechism and learned those precepts and values that make one's faith sure and strong.

From the moment of our marriage in 1962, we sought to establish a firm foundation for our family and we based those family values on how we were taught. We were blessed in having parents and grandparents with a rich tradition of strong family values. Our families saw the strength a solid family life brings to each member of a family.

Starting with our marriage in 1962, God gave us unquestionably the best and most glorious family. We came to appreciate the value of family through those values, faith, and culture passed down by our parents, who no doubt also copied the family model from their parents and grandparents.

Happy family living is founded on biblical principles. Some of the best advice comes from Paul in several of his letters. Just look at these excerpts dealing with family relationships:

> **Wives, submit to your husbands, as is fitting in the Lord. (Ephesians 5:22)**
>
> **Husbands, love your wives and do not be harsh with them. (Colossians 3:19)**
>
> **Children, obey your parents in everything, for this pleases the Lord. (Colossians 3:20)**
>
> **Fathers, do not embitter your children, or they will become discouraged. (Colossians 3:21)**
>
> **Wives, in the same way be submissive to your husbands so that, if any of them do not believe the word, they may be won over without words by the behavior of their wives, when they see the purity and reverence of your lives. Your beauty should not come from outward adornment, such as braided hair and the wearing of gold jewelry and fine clothes. Instead, it should be that of your inner self, the unfading beauty of a gentle and quiet spirit, which is of great worth in God's sight. For this is the way the holy women of the past who put their hope in God used to make themselves beautiful. They were submissive to their own**

husbands, like Sarah, who obeyed Abraham and called him her master. You are her daughters if you do what is right and do not give way to fear. Husbands, in the same way be considerate as you live with your wives, and treat them with respect as the weaker partner and as heirs with you of the gracious gift of life, so that nothing will hinder your prayers. (1 Peter 3:1–7)

Listen to your father, who gave you life, and do not despise your mother when she is old. (Proverbs 23:22)

The father of a righteous man has great joy; he who has a wise son delights in him. May your father and mother be glad; may she who gave you birth rejoice! (Proverbs 23:24–25)

Houses and wealth are inherited from parents, but a prudent wife is from the Lord. (Proverbs 19:14)

Children's children are a crown to the aged, and parents are the pride of their children. (Proverbs 17:6)

A family is a source of strength and rest. A family is a source of love, encouragement, and nurture. You will someday be called to establish your own family and to take on the responsibility of nurturing children, of encouraging each other as husband and wife and/or displaying love to those in your household. You may not marry and that is understandable. But the love and strength of the family unit should be available to you from your siblings and those who nurtured you along the way. Our dear children, we ask that you cherish the richness of a family founded in the spiritual knowledge of Jesus Christ. We encourage you to put all petty grievances behind and forgive those near and dear to you. Your family should be, and will be, a source of strength when you are down. A family will be a source of comfort in time of loss. And a family will be there when all others will forget you and leave you.

As Opa found throughout life, our family, wife, children, and grandchildren were the hope here on earth that provided the underpinning for bearing the hurts and pains of worldly affairs. God saw to it that we were blessed with riches far greater than gold or silver. God saw that our blessings came from heartfelt love and caring that only a God-fearing family can provide. And for that, Oma and Opa are grateful to you, your parents, and our parents for all the support and love we received during the years. Now it's your turn to pass it on. Do it joyfully and lovingly. And reap the riches that are there for you to enjoy.

CHAPTER 21

Honesty

Kings take pleasure in honest lips; they value a man who speaks the truth. (Proverbs 16:13)

Honesty is one of those foundational values that are essential for any civilized society to function well. One would think that in a book of virtues and legacies, particularly based on biblical values, there would be no need for a section on honesty. We would tend to think that anybody and everybody who has a foundation founded on faith, hope, and love would naturally practice a life of honesty. But the fact is no matter whether your friends, associates, fellow church members, or family are strong adherents to God's commandments, dishonesty prevails in every family, every neighborhood, every organization, every country, every ethnic group, and anywhere humans interact with other humans.

Honesty is a human virtue, which springs from deep in the heart. Man's hearts were originally born with inherent honesty, but sin changed all that. This discourse is not intended to discuss the psychological reasons for dishonesty, or the factors that encourage dishonesty. Sin is enough of an explanation and any attempt to explain it away with psychological theories is an exercise for the secular academics. The fact is that dishonesty is all too prevalent in our society and our everyday life. The book of Proverbs is filled with statements addressing dishonesty, and the pitfalls that result from a life built upon cheating and deception. Just look at the following passages:

Do not steal. Do not lie. Do not deceive one another. (Leviticus 19:11)

You must have accurate and honest weights and measures, so that you may live long in the land the Lord your God is giving you. For the Lord your God detests anyone who does these things, anyone who deals dishonestly. (Deuteronomy 25:15–16)

We will talk in a moment about the hurts, pains, and disappointments that emanate from friends, associates, and other acquaintances when dishonesty is practiced. Before we do that, we need to focus our attention on our own behavior and honesty. There is no need to point the finger or analyze the behavior of others when our own behavior is clouded in questionable practices.

You have been raised in an environment whereby dishonesty should not be difficult to define, let alone understand. Whatever the law of the land states, there are those situations that are outright dishonest and a violation of God's laws. If you are refunded too much cash in a grocery store, your honesty and heart should drive you to return the overage immediately. To our knowledge, there are no laws in the land now that state you must refund the overage in our example. But certainly God's commands say that you must, since you were never entitled to that excess in the first place. Honesty says that you must return what is not yours. If you are in business, and a customer mistakenly pays the same invoice twice, honesty says you will immediately refund the duplicate payment. If your employer makes a mistake on your paycheck and compensates you for too many hours, your duty and honesty dictates you bring the error to your employer's attention.

He who walks righteously and speaks what is right, who rejects gain from extortion and keeps his hand from accepting bribes, who stops his ears against plots of murder and shuts his eyes against contemplating evil—this is the man who will dwell on the heights, whose refuge will be the mountain fortress. His bread will be supplied, and water will not fail him. (Isaiah 33:15–16)

Wholesome, forthright behavior is a part of the natural personality, which God created in the first man. However, the result of sin brought with it a whole host of sinful behaviors. Dishonesty ranks right up there with the most heinous sins. The Bible does not refrain from disclosing and displaying the dishonest acts of the patriarchs of the Judeo-Christian faith. One only has to look at the dishonesty of Abraham or Jacob or David and come away with an appreciation that dishonesty plagues the hearts and minds of the most God-fearing.

You will notice that dishonesty always seems to run hand in hand with other evil behaviors. Lying about a past employment situation usually goes together with an embezzlement, a violation of work rules, or likely a sexual misbehavior. Dishonest money transactions always seem to go with bad investments, excessive spending, or support of a lifestyle incompatible with the will of the Lord.

Sometime in life, you will meet individuals who have a difficult time defining honesty or dishonesty. Those same individuals will usually rewrite the rules as their behavior dictates. In our freewheeling culture, far too many political, religious, or business leaders seem to have an inability to elucidate precisely what is dishonest. Whatever you can get away with is the norm of acceptable behavior.

The Bible shows that dishonesty was the first deception played by man on himself, and then tried to play on God. Notice what Eve did when tempted by Satan. She lied about why she did it and tried to blame Satan, but failed to acknowledge the evil of her own heart. Then Adam, in like manner, sought to blame the woman when confronted by God.

No sin permeates every other sin more than that of dishonesty, lying, or cheating. Look around you and see how often someone (even ourselves) has gotten into deep predicaments all because it started with a lie, a deception, or a dishonest act.

Whether in our family life, our business life, our school activities, our vocations, or even our church life, honesty is a foundation that is necessary for the conduct of fair and Christ-like initiatives. Dishonesty, on the other hand, breeds suspicion, distrust, envy, malice, and a host of other sins. After a while, the basis of the original sin is forgotten and consequences take over, leading to a quagmire of devastating and long-suffering results.

Surprisingly to most people is the complete honesty with which the Bible portrays dishonesty. Several of the following stories throughout the Old Testament (also listed is an example from the New Testament) portray acts of dishonesty and the ramifications resulting thereof:

- Story of Cain and Able (Genesis 4:8–16)
  o Murder and then lying to God

- Story of Aachen and Ai (Joshua 7)
  o Stealing and defying God's command
- Story of David and Bathsheba (2 Samuel 11)
  o Adultery, murder, and covetousness
- Story of Elisha's servant, Gehazi (2 Kings 5)
  o Greed, covetousness, and lying
- Story of Ananias and Sapphira (Acts 5:1–11)
  o Greed, covetousness, and lying

Let your life exhibit honesty and fairness. There are no rewards great enough to warrant dishonesty and deception. Your good name is a treasure and an asset. A pattern of dishonesty and devious behavior will plague you for most of your life. Not only is dishonesty wrong and against God's law, dishonesty smears your character and disgraces your reputation, and likely that of your family as well. As a Christian, you are set apart for a reward far greater than dishonesty can ever yield. Play fair with your fellow human beings, and be satisfied with what the Lord has endowed you. No gain ever gotten from dishonesty will gain the reward of eternal life.

Do not lie to each other, since you have taken off your old self with its practices and have put on the new self, which is being renewed in knowledge in the image of its Creator. (Colossians 3:9–10)

Do not take advantage of each other, but fear your God. I am the Lord your God. (Leviticus 25:17)

Honesty and fair play are the hallmarks of a Christian. Dishonesty is probably the easiest sin for Satan to entice any human being. All dishonesty starts out with a little sin. That sin doesn't seem to hurt anybody. Then the same deception is needed in short order to cover up the next deception. Then the habit of dishonesty becomes an easily practiced behavior. Before you know it, the deceiver deceives himself and no longer recognizes his dishonesty. It's a fabric of his personality; it becomes a natural inclination of his heart.

Pray always that you will not be enticed by the temptations of Satan. Ask the Lord to give you the power to resist the devil and stand strong against his urgings to deceive. The Lord will surely hold you up and give you the strength to overcome.

CHAPTER 22

Friends

So Jonathon made a covenant with the house of David, saying, "May the Lord call David's enemies to account." And Jonathon had David reaffirm his oath out of love for him, because he loved him as he loved himself. (1 Samuel 20:16–17)

As we have journeyed through life, God has blessed us with so much, and we have so many blessings for which to thank our God—blessings of food, nature, employment, freedom to worship, health, family, the Bible.

Take time to count your blessings. Right up there with the other blessings is one too often not appreciated. That blessing is the friendship of people we have come to fellowship with, confide with, worship with, and share with. During our lifetime, we have enjoyed friends who have been near and dear to us. There were those who have been there in time of need, those who have shared our joys, and those who have shared our sorrows.

Yet, over a lifetime, friends change and new friends appear. If you have moved from where you were raised as a child or changed physical locations during your formal education or employment, the likelihood of keeping long-term friends is more uncertain compared with maintaining a presence in one community during an entire lifetime. Some friends are with you for a while, but their lives take them elsewhere. Others are there for a lifetime. Today's modes of communication and the social networking sites of the Internet are making it easier to keep in touch with friends no matter where they are located.

Beginning early in life, we all launch our life's journey with friends. At a young age, much of our non-family daily life is shaped and occupied by and with friends. We have friends at school, we have friends in our neighborhood, and we have friends at our church. Later we have friends at college, we have friends at work, we have friends at our service organizations, and we have friends back in our neighborhoods. Yes, friends surround us very much during our lives. And the kind of friends we make begins to say a lot about ourselves and about what we are likely to become. Friends shape our thinking. Friends add to our knowledge. Friends comfort us and heal our hurts.

Wounds from a friend can be trusted, but an enemy multiplies kisses. (Proverbs 27:6)

Friends can be a valuable resource in time of need and sorrow, but friends can also hurt us. Friends can disappoint and betray us. They can manipulate and cause us mental and economic pain. They can lead us astray and take us far from the path God meant for us to walk.

He who walks with the wise grows wise, but a companion of fools suffers harm. (Proverbs 13:20)

You will become close with many people throughout life. Friends can be a rich source of comfort and support when needs arise. Conversely, real friends need your love and support and look to you for strength or guidance in times of great difficulty. For many years, we sought to be a healing comfort to people who were going through difficult periods in their lives. When people lost their jobs, they would seek counsel on what to do and where to go for help. We would listen and offer our help. We would give them leads and possible places to look for new employment.

You may ask, where should I look to nurture true friends? What characteristics mark a true friend? Then, how can I be a true friend, a person of faith and love, and one who is ready and willing to build up my fellow human colleague?

Therefore as God's chosen people, holy and dearly loved, clothe yourselves with compassion, kindness, humility, gentleness and patience. Bear with each other and forgive

whatever grievances you may have against one another. Forgive as the Lord forgave you. And over all these virtues put on love, which binds them all together in perfect unity. Let the peace of Christ rule in your hearts, since as members of one body you were called to peace. And be thankful. Let the word of Christ dwell in you richly as you teach and admonish one another with all wisdom, and as you sing psalms, hymns, and spiritual songs with gratitude in your hearts to God. And whatever you do, whether in word or deed, do it all in the name of the Lord Jesus, giving thanks to God the Father through him. (Colossians 3:12–17)

Let's take the first question. Where should I look to nurture true friends? We can get to this point from different directions. Your church is a very likely first start. If your church is a Bible-believing, Christ-centered church filled with vibrancy and a quest for evangelism, it is likely a valuable resource. But unless you are actively engaged in the mission of the church, are actively involved in the activities of the church, and are deep into the fellowship of believers, you are not going to nurture strong relationships with fellow Christians, and brothers and sisters of mutual understandings. A true friend is likely to be one who is of the same spirit and mind as you are (or should be). They should be tireless in their quest for a deeper practice of their faith and for a greater closeness to Jesus Christ. They should show by their lifestyle that Christ is first in their lives. Worldly pursuits, pursuit for material possessions, and gratification should be far from their minds. They should have a caring spirit and a compassionate heart. And they should be confidential about things you discuss or share. Christian friends are one of the most priceless assets you will possess in life; they require nurturing, they require investment, and they require care.

As the Father has loved me, so have I loved you. Now remain in my love. If you obey my commands, you will remain in my love, just as I have obeyed my Father's commands and remain in his love. I have told you this so that my joy may be in you and that your joy may be complete. My command is this: Love each other as I have loved you. Greater love has no one than this, that he lay down his life for his friends. You are my friends if you do what I command. I no longer call

you servants, because a servant does not know his master's business. Instead, I have called you friends, for everything that I learned from my Father I have made known to you. You did not choose me, but I chose you and appointed you to go and bear fruit—fruit that will last. Then the Father will give you whatever you ask in my name. This is my command: Love each other. (John 15:9–17)

Let's develop a response to the second question we posed. What characteristics mark a true friend? Well, we just named a couple in the preceding paragraph but others come to mind.

- Can they keep your confidential things confidential?
- Do they want something other than your friendship?
- Do they want to borrow money?
- Are they there only in times of prosperity?

Like a bad tooth or a lame foot is reliance on the unfaithful in times of trouble. (Proverbs 25:19)

- Is Christ's love and Christ-like foundational principles at the forefront of their advice during times of comfort and need?
- Do they want something that you have—your house, your husband, your wife, your job, or a job with your company?
- Do they build your faith?
- Are they a support in time of need?
- Do your friends help you grow in the knowledge and wisdom of the Lord?
- Are your friends concerned about your spiritual well-being, about your destiny?

As we said before, such friends are most likely to come from your church. While many work environments provide a healthy Christ-centered structure, the most likely place to develop long lasting, supportive friendships is in the body of Christ the church.

A righteous man is cautious in friendship, but the way of the wicked leads them astray. (Proverbs 12:26)

A man of many companions may come to ruin, but there is a friend who sticks closer than a brother. (Proverbs 18:24)

The Book of Virtues by William J. Bennett is a must-read for a whole variety of reasons. The book is a masterpiece on many aspects of the virtues of life, as we are codifying them here. He is far more eloquent than we are in characterizing friendship virtues, and for that reason, take some time to read that book and glean its lessons and words of wisdom. Bennett has this to say about friendships and bogus friendships:

> *Friendship usually rises out of mutual interests and common aims, and these pursuits are strengthened by the benevolent impulses that sooner or later grow. The demands of friendship—for frankness, for self-revelation, for taking friends' criticisms as seriously as their expressions of admiration or praise, from stand-by-me loyalty, and for assistance to the point of self-sacrifice—are all potent encouragements to moral maturation and even ennoblement.*

> *Of course, weaknesses induce companionship just as easily, in fact more easily, than do virtues. There are relationships undeserving of the title friendship that go by that name nonetheless, the kinds of "friendship" English essayist Joseph Addison called "confederacies in vice, or leagues of pleasure." Mutual desires and selfishness can be foundations of counterfeit friendships. In our age, when casual acquaintance often comes so easily, and when intimacy comes too soon and too cheaply, we need to be reminded that genuine friendships take time. They take effort to make, and work to keep. Friendship is a deep thing. It is, indeed, a form of love. And while it may be, as C. S. Lewis said, the least biological form of love, it is also one of the most important.*

John Bunyan's *Pilgrim's Progress* is the absolute must-read sometime during your life. It was a favorite of Opa's mother and has become a special favorite of Oma and Opa. Early on in the journey of Christian, a supposed friend accompanies him by the name of Pliable. Pliable is more than a little mushy in his conviction for the Christian life and at the earliest opportunity in his short trek with Christian, he does a fast exit stage left when the going gets a little tough; some friend he is:

Now I saw in my dream that, just as they had ended this talk, they drew near to a very miry slough that was in the midst of the plain; and they being heedless, did both fall suddenly into the bog. The name of the slough was "Despond." Here, therefore, they wallowed for a time, being grievously bedaubed with the dirt; and CHRISTIAN, because of the burden that was on his back, began to sink in the mire.

Pli. *Then said PLIABLE, "Ah! neighbour CHRISTIAN, where are you now?"*

Chr. *"Truly," said CHRISTIAN, "I do not know."*

Pli. *At that PLIABLE began to be offended, and angrily said to his fellow, "Is this the happiness you have told me of all this while? If we have such ill speed at our first setting out, what may we expect 'twixt this and our journey's end? If I get out again with my life, you shall possess the brave country alone." And with that he gave a desperate struggle or two, and got out of the mire on that side of the slough which was next to his own house: so away he went, and CHRISTIAN saw him no more.*

Wherefore CHRISTIAN was left to tumble in the Slough of Despond alone; but still he endeavoured to struggle to that side of the slough that was farthest from his own house, and next to the wicket gate: which he did, but could not get out, because of the burden that was upon his back. But I beheld, in my dream, that a man came to him whose name was HELP, and asked him what he did there?

Chr. *"Sir," said CHRISTIAN, "I was bidden to go this way by a man called EVANGELIST, who directed me also to yonder gate, that I might escape the wrath to come; and as I was going thither, I fell in here."*

Help. *But why did you not look for the steps?*

Chr. *Fear followed me so hard, that I fled the next way and fell in.*

Help. *Then said he, "Give me thy hand." So he gave him his hand, and he drew him out; and set him upon some ground, and bade him go on his way.*

He lifted me out of the slimy pit, out of the mud and mire, he set my feet upon a rock, and gave me a firm place to stand. (Psalms 40:2)

So we say to you, nurture good friendships. Take care in picking good, wholesome friends. Make sure your friends are truly willing to ride with you through the bad times as well as the good times. Recognize that true friendship means giving and sharing. Be a friend to someone in need. They will likely be a friend for life.

CHAPTER 23

Your Body and Health

Do you not know that your body is a temple of the Holy Spirit, who is in you, whom you have received from God? You are not your own; you were bought at a price. Therefore honor God with your body. (1 Corinthians 6:19–20)

When work on this book began, Opa worked for a company owned by a British group. At that time, he was a member of the group's board of directors in London, England. This book started as a pastime during travel to and from those board meetings held in England. Traveling once a month during a fifteen-year period gave him plenty of time to meditate and jot down notes and ideas. Then, at age fifty-seven, Opa took a position as CEO of a Kalamazoo plastics company on whose board he had been serving for the previous nine years. Finally, retiring at age sixty and concluding the leadership of a capital campaign at Richland Bible Church in Michigan, a member of the church asked Opa to join a newly formed pharmaceutical drug research and discovery company. The company formed in late 2003 following a termination of the drug research organization of the former Pharmacia in downtown Kalamazoo.

As CEO of PharmOptima, it meant having to learn a new technology—microbiology, chemistry, kinetics, pharmacology, and the like. A wonderful group of men in the company (all senior research scientists) helped teach the basics of drug development and illustrated those basics in non-technical language so a novice (such as Opa) could understand them. Their patience and clarity of thought aided immeasurably in helping Opa get up to speed in the highly complex world of drug research, small molecules, AbsorptionDistributionMetabolismExcretion, gram-negative bacteria, and a host of other cell biology and microbiology terms and techniques.

In no time, we (Opa learning during the day and briefing Oma at night) became *educated* about health issues, germs, bacteria, viruses, and a host of other fascinating biological wonders. While thinking about this new career endeavor, the thought came to mind that we are called by God to be concerned with our physical bodies as much as we care for our spiritual bodies. While the condition of our spiritual body and soul is of paramount importance, we are commanded by God to look after the well-being of our physical flesh as well.

The book of Leviticus devotes much space to instructions for the people of Israel on how to maintain sanitary conditions of one's self and of the community. The language is instructional in nature, not scientific. God, in His wisdom, is preparing a people, who will be living in close proximity to one another, for a clean and healthy environment and one free of disabling and/or killing bacteria. After all, these people never would have survived the rigors of the desert trek were it not for strict adherence to sanitary practices.

When sin came into the world, it brought with it an attack on the spiritual body of mankind. With that same fall of man, came an attack on the physical body as well. The wage of sin became death and with it an end to the blissful, eternal, physical existence on earth. In many ways, this was a blessing, for it was not God's desire that we should remain as inhabitants on an earth corrupted by Satan. God in His infinite wisdom chose to provide a means for man to escape the wretchedness of this earthly sinful existence through the sacrifice of His Son, Jesus Christ, and allow man to be reunited with Him in an incorruptible body. But the physical body had now been set in motion to decay, to suffer pain, to be deformed, and to suffer ailments.

Throughout life, you will be afflicted with ailments, physical pains, irritants, and the like. You may also suffer far greater sickness and heartache, sicknesses that drain your energy and your spirit. During our lifetimes, we have been extremely blessed in that neither we, nor our children, nor our grandchildren have suffered from diseases that incapacitate or cripple the body or mind. While we have had our share of broken bones, heart problems, blood pressure problems, and the like, nothing has resulted in debilitating illnesses or incapacities. Our prayers have constantly been with those families who have seen children, parents, spouses, or grandchildren suffer from body-deforming, mind-impairing, or crippling diseases. We know not the reason why some people are struck and others are not. The medical research world continues to probe the reasons for such tragedies. Genetics is the current cutting-edge science seeking to learn the proclivity for some people to inherit mutations leading to crippling ailments. We marvel at the science and encourage men and women to continue research into finding medicines to heal and cure the many dreadful diseases that torment mankind.

Through it all, do know and remember one thing: God does not bring these diseases or infirmities! Sin brought these into the world. Satan is fully and wholly responsible for the entire problem. We were created perfect. When our first father and mother sinned, all the consequences of that sin came raining down on us brought about by none other than Satan himself.

We need to make sure we are doing everything possible to maintain a healthy, functioning body. To the extent that we have the ability to maintain and improve our well-being, God calls us to lead a life honoring and nourishing to the physical body. The following passage from Psalms gives assurance to the faithful and comfort to those who trust in God.

He who dwells in the shelter of the Most High will rest in the shadow of the Almighty. I will say of the Lord, "He is my refuge and my fortress, my God, in whom I trust. Surely he will save you from the fowler's snare and from the deadly pestilence. He will cover you with his feathers, and under his wings you will find refuge; his faithfulness will be your shield and rampart. You will not fear the terror of night, nor the arrow that flies by day, nor the pestilence that stalks in the darkness, nor the plague that destroys at midday. A thousand may fall at your side, ten thousand at your right hand, but it will not come near you. You will only observe with your eyes and see the punishment of the wicked.

"If you make the Most High your dwelling—even the Lord, who is my refuge—then no harm will befall you, no disaster will come near your tent. For he will command his angels concerning you to guard you in all your ways; they will lift you up in their hands, so that you will not strike your foot

against a stone. You will tread upon the lion and the cobra; you will trample the great lion and the serpent. 'Because he loves me,' says the Lord, 'I will rescue him; I will protect him, for he acknowledges my name.

"'He will call upon me, and I will answer him; I will be with him in trouble, I will deliver him and honor him. With long life will I satisfy him and show him my salvation.'" (Psalm 91)

Your body is a magnificent creation with a complexity far beyond the comprehension of man. As we research the workings of the cells, bacteria, the brain, and the heart, any doctor or researcher will tell you that the more we come to learn about the body's workings, the more intriguing are its mysteries. The elegance with which the eye or the heart, let alone the brain, are fashioned is nothing short of miraculous. The details of the nervous system or the immune system hold mysteries well beyond current comprehension. Only God could have created such a finely tuned system of interacting activities.

Dr. Stephen C. Meyer wrote a wonderful book on the subject of the human cell and DNA titled, *Signature in the Cell*. The work by Dr. Meyer is intense and revealing. In short, you will see the absolute elegance of the workings of DNA and RNA and the fact that only a great God and Creator could have created mankind. We highly recommend this book for your study into the workings of the human body.

As Christians, we are charged with doing everything in our power to maintain healthy bodies and minds. Some things are not within our power to control; however, other things are within our power. While the body is durable and capable of putting up a strong fight when attacked, some activities are simply *more destructive* and *more suddenly* fatal than others are. Your body was not made to be abused. There are limits to the punishment or abuse to which you can subject your body and mind. Consider the following:

- Poison kills instantaneously; alcohol abuse takes more time.
- Inhaling CO (carbon monoxide) is immediately fatal; inhaling cigarette smoke is slower to kill.

- Reckless driving can result in instant death; a lethargic, sedate lifestyle can take years to take its toll.
- A blow to the head with a hammer can lead to immediate death; continuous battering of the head from boxing can take a slower, but no less surer, toll.
- Excessive weight gain will negatively affect your overall health and well-being.
- Depression, unless treated, will lead to debilitating physical ailments and eventual early death.
- Stress has an eroding effect on the body, and recent research is pointing to a causative relationship between stress and a host of crippling and life-threatening diseases.

So there are things you can do to maintain good health. But by the same token, we are commanded not to be so preoccupied with our bodies that they become an idol to our lives and lifestyle. While care for our health and well-being is important, *excess* attention to the appearance or physique of these earthly bodies will surely distract us from the greater attention, which needs to be given to our spiritual bodies. Simply ask yourself if you are devoting more time to the maintenance of your spiritual body or to your physical body. Look at your calendar and make note of the time each week you spend in spiritual conditioning versus physical conditioning. Be honest with yourself. Is a six-hour round of golf matched by a six-hour study of Jeremiah? Is a five-time a week, one-hour visit to the health club matched by a five-hour visit to the sick, the elderly, the lonely, the hurting, or the imprisoned? Is a seven-hour boating and swimming outing matched by a seven-hour study of the Bible or ministry to the lost in your city? You get the point. Unless we are seriously challenging the body we are trying to nurture, Satan will always incline our thoughts and desires to that which emphasizes the physical and negates the spiritual.

A long life is something to cherish and enjoy. Healthful living is important in keeping your mind and body sound. In today's world, life expectancy is advancing, and we will very likely be living a third of our life after age sixty. While very few can enjoy the vigorous and rigorous activity we once enjoyed in our younger years, there are many opportunities to keep the mental body in sharp working order. While regular exercise is essential for elderly folk, so too is an active mind, assuring that we are not letting the brain erode due to lack of exercise. With a rapid increase in the incidence of Alzheimer's disease and dementia among the elderly, we need to make sure that our elders (and that includes Oma and Opa) are mentally active and involved in activities that give them purpose and a sense of contribution.

Ecclesiastes 12 sums it up wisely and beautifully. You may not appreciate the full meaning of these verses until you pass forty or fifty, but read them and learn from them. While you are still young and vibrant, use your healthy bodies to work diligently in the promotion and advancement of God's kingdom, for there will come a time when your bodies will wear out and you will no longer have the energy to engage in the activities you once were so capable of.

> **Remember your Creator in the days of your youth, before the days of trouble come and the years approach when you will say,**
>
> **"I find no pleasure in them"—**
> **before the sun and the light and the moon and the stars grow dark,**
> **and the clouds return after the rain;**
>
> **when the keepers of the house tremble, and the strong men stoop,**
> **when the grinders cease because they are few,**
> **and those looking through the windows grow dim;**
>
> **when the doors to the street are closed and the sound of grinding fades; when men rise up at the sound of birds, but all their songs grow faint;**
>
> **when men are afraid of heights and of dangers in the streets; when the almond tree blossoms and the grasshopper drags himself along and desire no longer is stirred. Then man goes to his eternal home and mourners go about the streets.**
>
> **Remember him—before the silver cord is severed, or the golden bowl is broken; before the pitcher is shattered at the spring, or the wheel broken at the well, and the dust returns**

to the ground it came from, and the spirit returns to God who gave it.

"Meaningless! Meaningless!" says the Teacher. "Everything is meaningless!"

Yes, life has a way of eating away at our mortal bodies. Everything mortal eventually decays and returns to dust, but our souls are ever alive. Our souls are the essence of our body. Your soul is the body part that you need to nurture, grow, and prepare. Your soul will never wear out. It bridges the gap between the living world and the eternal, spiritual world. Your soul, which was knitted by God long before time began, will last for eternity, never to be extinguished or eliminated. While you are here in the temporal world, God demands you care for the physical body so that it is a healthy and sound temple for the soul to reside. Care for your bodies and make sure that you are doing everything to make them sound and beautiful for the Lord.

CHAPTER 24

Work

Lazy hands make a man poor, but diligent hands bring wealth. (Proverbs 10:4)

Life begins so innocently as a baby and as an adolescent. Parents, grandparents, and those near and dear to us provide our every need. We are nurtured, fed, protected, and loved. We are kept safe, kept warm, taught, and trained. Our environment is safe and non-competitive.

But as we mature into our teen years, we begin to feel the pressure of having to make it on our own. While parents guide and instruct us, we are ever so slowly, but surely, required to be responsible for our own well-being. Learning to walk, learning to talk, learning to ride a bike, and learning to obey school authorities all begin to establish the foundation for a life of work.

Work plays a key role in the foundation of our lives. It gives us joy, yet frustration. It gives us sustenance, yet temptation. It develops relationships, yet can potentially guide us astray. Work gives us the feeling of self-worth and dignity, but at the same time can strip us of that very same self-worth and dignity. The choice you make about your career or work calling will have a profound influence on your innermost feelings of joy and contentment. And over the course of your adult years, virtually every other aspect of your life will trace its attitude back to your outlook on and satisfaction with your work.

First, your relationship with God will be influenced by the joy you feel in your career. We should make it clear at the outset that when we speak of work, we not only refer to a vocation outside the home. Work as we reference here can just as well refer to those mothers who choose to rear their children at home, who provide homeschooling, or who choose to compliment their husband's undertakings with a home presence to nurture the home environment faithfully.

If a man is lazy, the rafters sag; if his hands are idle, the house leaks. (Proverbs 10:18)

I went past the field of the sluggard, past the vineyard of the man who lacks judgment; thorns had come up everywhere, the ground was covered with weeds, and the stone wall was in ruins. I applied my heart to what I observed and learned a lesson from what I saw: a little sleep, a little slumber, a little folding of the hands to rest—and poverty will come on you like a bandit and scarcity like an armed man. (Proverbs 24:30–34)

As you near the end of your grammar education (today that is twelfth grade in high school), you are called rather quickly to begin thinking about the path you will pursue for your life's endeavor. In some cases, you will follow in a career that your parents or grandparents had or have pursued. Your grandfather or grandmother may have been a physician, and so you feel the calling to that field. Or, your father or mother may have pursued a career in sales, or accounting, or community service. You may possibly see that as a path you would enjoy.

No matter what career path you are considering, let us strongly suggest that you first take it to the Lord in prayer. For surely, God has a plan for you, and He already knows the path He will have you go. So it only makes sense to reach up to Him and ask Him to guide you in your deliberations and your search. God will always plant the right answer in the mind of a Christian. You will always make the right choice when God has been asked for His guidance.

My son, if you accept my words and store up my commands within you, turning your ear to wisdom and applying your heart to understanding, and if you call out for insight and cry aloud for understanding, and if you look for it as for silver and search for it as for hidden treasure, then you will

> **understand the fear of the LORD and find the knowledge of God. For the LORD gives wisdom, and from his mouth come knowledge and understanding. (Proverbs 2:1–6)**

The first step in planning your future is to take the decision to God. That decision may involve deciding to continue your formal education by going on to college. The decision may be to pursue a career that *initially* does not require a college education, such as a mechanic, plumber, painter, electrician, gardener, or a career in the military. We say *initially* because every pursuit in life will eventually require more education and training. Timing and choice of vocations are the issues here. But let us give you a valuable piece of advice. Higher education is always far easier and more effectively pursued immediately after grammar education or high school. Young minds far more easily grasp facts, concepts, and ideas of subjects at an early age. Attention span and the ability to remember become more difficult with age. And continuing with your formal education right after high school is more likely to get you to complete the higher education without the temptations to stay out of school should you decide to work a few years.

So now being in your twenties, you have chosen a life's endeavor, you have completed your formal education, and you are now ready for the full-time work world.

> **Lazy hands make a man poor, but diligent hands bring wealth. (Proverbs 10:4)**

As you begin your work experience, give your very best. Honor and respect your employer. Take joy in your work. Be faithful to your assignments. Be punctual. Be loyal. Respect your employer's property and trade secrets. Thank your employer for the opportunity to be a part of the business or organization. Learn as much as you can. Decide early on that you will be the very best in your chosen field. Listen to the advice of those older than you and be discerning in your selection of mentors. Learn, develop, and grow. And always thank the Lord for giving you the health and mind to be a good employee.

> **All hard work brings a profit, but mere talk leads only to poverty. (Proverbs 14:23)**

Then there will come a time when you will begin to assess if the position you are in or the company you are employed is right for you. Changing careers or changing jobs is an important decision. Have you asked the Lord to speak to you? Has He opened a door for you? Are you doing it for selfish reasons or is the change positioning you for a better opportunity in the Lord's service? In assessing this decision, ask yourself a few questions about your current situation and the new situation:

- Is my current position enriching? Am I witnessing?
- Does the current position support your family? Will the new one?
- Does the current position give you dignity? Will the new one?
- Does either position put you in association with God-spirited people? Are they uplifting to your faith and walk with God? Or is it a position likely leading you to drift from your foundational faith?

In making job or career changes, be careful that you are not developing a reputation as a job-jumper. So many times, we have seen those individuals who have a work history as long as your arm, never seeming to stay in one position for more than a year or two. To future employers, such an individual looks to be one who is unstable, cannot handle the interaction of other people as soon as the newness of a job wears off, or just lacks "stick-to-itiveness." Be sure that your career moves reflect consistency and commitment. Hang in there when the going gets tough. Every job has its time of boredom and tension. Every occupation has its elements of frustration and conflict. Every job has its jerk to contend with, but stay committed and determined to your work. Always seek the help and counsel of the Lord. You will be amazed how many frustrations and obstacles evaporate when you ask God to carry the burden for you.

Ecclesiastes 5:18–20 is a beautiful statement on the place of work in a person's life:

> **Then I realized that it is good and proper for a man to eat and drink, and to find satisfaction in his toilsome labor under the sun during the few days of life God has given him—for this is his lot. Moreover, when God gives any man wealth and possessions, and enables him to enjoy**

them, to accept his lot and be happy in his work—this is a gift of God. He seldom reflects on the days of his life, because God keeps him occupied with gladness of heart. (Ecclesiastes 5:18-20)

We discussed earlier the importance of keeping a balance in life. That is ever so true when work, family, and worship are competing for your time. Here, we want to address the issue of balancing work with worship. Depending on the occupation you have pursued, your work time will compete with your worship time, and that competition will be more or less intense. Every person alive has experienced balancing work with worship. We did, and there never comes an end to the potential for letting work interfere with your worship life. There will always be a reason to postpone Sabbath worship to the next week.

You need to establish, develop, and nurture a firm discipline so you place worship ahead of work. Opa well knows the pressures to yield a Sunday or two to work. Having lead four companies during his career, he found there was never enough time in the workweek to get everything done. There were always project deadlines to meet. There were always piles of reports or papers to read. And there were always the reasons to visit outlying facilities and business associates. But believe us; trying to use the Sabbath to get caught up is never the answer. There will always be another list of unfinished business issues to attend to, no matter how many hours you devote to your job. Make a point early on in your career that nothing will detract from your time of worship, least of all your job. It isn't worth it!

We need to talk a moment about life expectancy and work careers, or more to the point, second careers. It is a fact that most people are living longer and are generally healthier than those who lived seventy to one hundred years ago. For our entire working lives, people generally worked until age sixty-two or sixty-five, and then retired to a life of rest and relaxation. When Social Security was enacted, retirement age was set at sixty-five. The life expectancy of a man at that time was about sixty-seven or sixty-eight. The entire funding of Social Security was predicated on the assumption that a working person would only draw on the system for a few years. It was intended to provide the few remaining years of a person's life with an income that could carry him or her through to death, likely two to four years.

Well, that has all changed. The retirement age for full benefits has been raised to about seventy years, but the life expectancy has risen to eighty or more years. First, people should expect and plan to work longer than their parents did, and they should plan to save enough to supplement their retirement income for what could be a much-extended period of reduced income. In years gone by, you worked for forty-five years, retired, and lived for three more years. Today, you work for forty-five years, retire, and live for twenty or twenty-five more years.

So, the point of the matter is to make sure you are putting something away for the day when retirement arrives. (We mention that in the next chapter on money.) Retirement can span a good number of years. You should plan and ready yourself for either an extended period of five years in the vocation you already have, or plan on a second or a third work career. We are seeing this unfold in our day. People are taking up new endeavors after they retire from their regular career. Opa did exactly that when at the age of sixty-one, he collaborated with a group of scientists to start a life sciences contract research company that serves the pharmaceutical industry. You, likewise, will get to that point in life when your regular work career will end, but your mind and health are such that you are not ready to cease your daily labors. If the Lord gives you the health and the ability to continue to be a contributor to His kingdom, be prepared to step up, answer His call, and serve where He sends you. Oma and Opa have looked at these years as equally enriching and enjoyable as we did our younger years of career pursuit. Oh, be sure the compensation isn't the same nor the energy is quite what it used to be, but the opportunities for witness, counsel, and sharing are unbelievable. We see these years as a way to impart our experiences and counsel with the next generation and show what God can do in the life of a family blessed with health and prosperity.

The writer in Proverbs sums up our final piece of advice:

Commit to the Lord whatever you do, and your plans will succeed. (Proverbs 16:3)

CHAPTER 25

Money

The love of money is the root of all evil. (Corinthians 6:19–20)

We probably should have started this book with this chapter, because money underpins so many of life's undertakings. So many of life's sorrows, conflicts, and pains find their roots or their origins in the love of or the lack of money. There is never enough of it, it never seems to be in the right people's hands, it never seems to be there when we really need it, and there never seems to be a way to get more of it. Whether in marriage, work, church, school, or society, money is always the limiting, moderating, or braking mechanism. Money is always the element that gets in the way and slows things down. Ideas are abundant and plentiful, and solutions are clever and artful—if only we had enough money to get us there.

A feast is made for laughter, and wine makes life merry, but money is the answer for everything. (Ecclesiastes 10:19)

As you read this chapter, we are assuming you are living, or have spent the majority of your life, in the United States or Europe. The Western world today has enjoyed abundance unknown throughout the history of mankind. Our citizens are well fed, housed in comfortable homes, able to transport on well-maintained roads, have first-rate education available to the broad masses, and health care is the best. We have material possessions beyond imagination: computers, boats, cycles, vacations, lawnmowers, and fashionable clothes adorned with elegant jewelry. We have VCRs and DVDs (what new gadgets do you have today that we never dreamt of?), furniture, personal beauty services to improve our physical appearances, and on and on. We travel internationally with ease and comfort—breakfast in London, lunch over Greenland, and dinner in Chicago—all in the same day. When it comes to personal comforts, we lack nothing. When you stop to think about it, money is not the limiting factor. Allocation or prioritization of that money is really the issue.

Money is the medium that drives all of this and other things as well. Some are for good, but far too many are things that merely pacify our personal wants and desires. There are far too many traps to attract our money. We fall into so many temptations to want things, things that in the end never really satisfy or enrich. We yearn for so much that is transient and fleeting.

Yet, on a more positive and constructive note, money builds churches, it builds hospitals, and it builds and equips centers for the poor and homeless. Money builds homes for the elderly, it builds Christian schools, and it builds shelters for the abused. Money feeds the hungry in far-off lands. Money spreads the Gospel and trains ministers and missionaries. Money defends our freedom to worship and live in a land free from oppression. Yes, money has attributes that can grace us with blessings and bind us closer to God.

A stingy man is eager to get rich and is unaware that poverty awaits him. (Proverbs 28:22)

From the preceding, you can see that money is the blood that nourishes and drives a system for good or for bad. Money commands power and prestige. Money is the salve of the mercy-givers as much as it is the opium of the evildoers. What we do with our (actually, it is God's) money says everything about who we are and where our values lie.

So what is your outlook on money? How do you view money? Has your life been excessively driven by the pursuit of money? Have you sought a profession solely for garnering more money? Have you and your family let money become the focus of your entire reason for existence? Has money become the vehicle driving you?

Two things I ask of you, O Lord; do not refuse me before I die: Keep falsehood and lies far from me; give me neither poverty nor riches, but give me only my daily bread.

> **Otherwise, I may have too much and disown you and say, "Who is the Lord?" Or I may become poor and steal, and so dishonor the name of my God. (Proverbs 30:7–9)**

You should know that this malady is not unique to you or to your generation. Every generation from the beginning of mankind has wrestled with this conflict. Within the essence of money's utility lies the very foundation of its ability to corrupt and destroy.

Throughout our life, we wrestled with money issues and budgetary constraints. We experienced times of pressure and hopelessness. We felt pressure when the money never seemed to match our needs. Yet time and time again, upon careful and close examination, our needs were ever too frequently our wants. Too often, the social pressures or the sinful urges of satisfying our desires with money clouded us. Money seemed to be the yardstick by which success was measured or happiness was attained. The race was on and whoever got the most won. Money measured personal success. Money brought attention and a sense of power. Money was the sole means of keeping score. If you had it, you got attention. If a church had a lot of it, it built huge edifices to project its importance in the community. When a government had it, the leaders spent with reckless abandon. Money became, and still is, the force to attain power and influence.

> **Whoever loves money never has money enough; whoever loves wealth is never satisfied with his income. This too is meaningless. (Ecclesiastes 5:10)**

But in the process, it was so easy to forget God's desire for our lives, so easy to forget that God had other ideas for us. We forgot that on many occasions God gave us money as a way of testing our love for Him. We corrupted the purpose of money and made it our god.

We started out in our married life with barely enough money to put gas in the car each week. Going to college full time and working full time put constant pressure on our family and made our life one of constant struggle and challenge. Looking back now, those years were times of preparation and discipline. God knew exactly what we needed. God knew exactly how we were going to be provided for. Not one single time did God ever desert us or abandon us. Never were we in want or destitute.

Our needs and much, much more were always met and there was always money left over.

Then as the years went by, we began to be concerned about security. As if *money* would provide security. A most common affliction among people over the age of fifty is the fear of running out of money. We work for forty years and then begin to worry if there will be enough money to live on, or enough money to enjoy the things we sacrificed for along the way. Notice how the preoccupation with money slowly creates worry about existence—not looking to God, the provider of all good and perfect gifts. Did not God provide fully along the way? Do you think he would abandon you now?

> **Look at the birds of the air; they do not sow or reap or store away in barns, and yet your heavenly Father feeds them. Are you not much more valuable than they? (Matthew 6:26)**

We should mention that underlying our outlook on money was a firm foundation built on Christian instruction about the treatment of money. Throughout our lives, we were instructed in our schools, in our churches, and in our Christian service opportunities, that faithful stewardship of our financial resources was critical to our enjoyment of life on earth. We were taught that God was the giver of all good and perfect gifts, and we knew that those gifts belonged to Him first. We were mere stewards of what He had given us. Therefore, wise administration of those resources was the bedrock of our use of money.

> **My son, do not forget my teaching, but keep my commands in your heart, for they will prolong your life many years and bring you prosperity. (Proverbs 3:2)**

The Lord will provide for your needs as He sees fit. When times of financial stress seem to be eroding the foundation of life, go to the Lord in prayer. Take a good hard look at your priorities in life. Take a good look at your activities in day-to-day living. Ask these simple questions and then answer them honestly, and I mean very honestly:

- Has your prayer life been faithful and consistent?
- Has your church attendance been faithful?

- Has your tithing been faithful?
- Have you read the Bible daily and with a willingness to follow?
- Have you really been putting your trust in the Lord?
- Have you really had your life focused on, and dedicated to, the Lord's service? Or that of man?
- Has money become the "God" of your life?

How you answer these questions should give you a better insight as to why you never seem to have enough money or resources; how you answer these questions will tell you whether your life's compass is broken. If it is, you are likely off course and in need of a course correction. Get the compass fixed or replaced. Take a new bearing on your life's direction.

As you begin to take the responsibility of managing your personal financial affairs, you need to address those elements that constitute good stewardship. Space does not permit going into extensive detail about every aspect of money management, but let the following list provide a sampling of those matters we addressed and those that you will no doubt encounter:

o *Tithing*—No matter your income, first tithe to the Lord, and then learn to live off the remainder.

o *Saving*—Saving is a must. After tithing, put an amount away for yourself, for that rainy day, for that time when emergencies will arise, when you need a little extra to make a down payment on a home, or an emergency, or for that day when you will look at retirement.

o *Budgets*—Live within your means!

o *Generosity*—Share willingly with those in need. Don't let your Christian organizations suffer through lack of money.

o *Children*—Teach your children the wise use of money and the relationship between work and money.

o *Investment spending versus pleasure spending*—There is nothing wrong with pleasure spending, but be sure you are putting a tidy sum away for that day when you can no longer earn a living.

o *Loaning to family and strangers*—Tread carefully. Loaning to children and grandchildren is one thing; to other family members is something completely different.

o **Acknowledge that you may not know how to plan and manage your finances**—Get good help or advice.
o **Estate planning**—Bequests to children or grandchildren are things to think about down the road; be generous yet discerning.
o **Money in a marriage**—Separate handling of money is not a long-term healthy situation. If one member is *irresponsible* with money, solve the problem of joint money management rather than paper over the problem.

Another little piece of advice seems worthy at this point. Pay absolutely no attention to what your friends have or how they live. It is so easy to look at your close friends or your neighbors and wonder how they manage. How do they seem to have more than you do? How is it they seem to go on vacations, buy new cars, remodel their homes, or build a swimming pool? How do they seem to have it all?

Well, after a lifetime of such experiences, we learned long ago that things might not be what they seem. You are likely unaware of the estate left them by Grandpa or the monthly income from a privately held company. Worse yet, these so-called "lifestyle have-it-alls" may very possibly be up to their cheekbones in debt. They may be spending way beyond their means. They may be on the road to disaster and not know it. And in time, their house of cards will tumble tragically down around their ears, and you will have the opportunity to see the real life consequences of living for the material. As we are writing this, the world is going through a major readjustment of wealth. People who for too long have lived on excessive borrowing from their ever inflating home values are now in the midst of the greatest repossession effort known in more than one hundred years.

The lesson here is to manage your finances well, and live with what the Lord has given you. He knows your needs, and He will provide precisely what you need to live a life pleasing to Him and yet satisfying to yourself. Know your real income and budget accordingly. You can't spend what you don't have. In that vein, be very wise about the use of credit. Our best piece of advice is to use credit sparingly. Credit for a home is acceptable so long as the payments fit into a budget and that budget has recognized the inevitable contingencies of life. Books upon books are written on the wise, biblically based use of money and credit and we direct you to read those in the spirit of wisdom.

Now a few words about investments. As you begin to build that nest egg for the future, you will need the Wisdom of Solomon to not only build that nest egg, but to protect it in the first place. The nature of life is such that painful financial catastrophes will happen. We are experiencing that right now in 2010 and 2011 with what started as a financial maelstrom in 2008 and is now leading to an evaporation of people's savings and retirement plans. Vast wealth has dissipated in the blink of an eye. We are hearing of trillions of dollars being lost in the housing and stock markets. American citizens are seeing their idols, founded on the so-called strength of the American financial system, drop on their faces during the middle of the night—so much for that rock-solid institution of security. You need to be wise and prudent with your savings. There are no get-rich quick schemes. If you are presented with one, know that in due course, it will become a get-poor quick result. When planning your investments, take the decision to the Lord. Ask Him to direct you to a wise advisor. Protect your principal first.

Many a person has been in a situation where money has been squandered. The story of the prodigal son is as much a story of wealth management as it is about God's rejoicing when a wayward child returns to the fold.

The younger son of a wealthy father decides it's time to enjoy the attributes of his inheritance. He asks for his inheritance in advance and goes off to live a life of reckless and wild behavior. Soon the wealth dissipates, and he is relegated to work on a farm feeding pigs. He returns to his father and pleads for forgiveness. The story ends with the father returning his son to the comfort and joy of his rightful home. Now, keep in mind that this son could return to his father. His father still enjoyed wealth and prosperity. The son then settled into a life likely filled with the comforts of monetary and life-comforting resources.

In your lives and ours, such a result may not be the result of squandering money. You may have blown it all and need to start from the bottom again. The lesson here is to be good stewards of what the Lord has entrusted you with the first time. Once lost, you may need to work countless years to return to the point before you squandered the savings you so faithfully worked for. Opa and Oma have been there, and the pain of regaining the lost wealth was severe. But the Lord continued to give us opportunities to regain our foothold once we acknowledged our unfaithfulness in being good stewards of what we had in the first place.

> Be sure you know the condition of your flocks, give careful attention to your herds; for riches do not endure forever, and a crown is not secure for all generations. (Proverbs 27:23–24)

One last thought before we conclude. Be wisely generous with the gifts God has given you. The needs of the poor are great. So many people in your own city have not been blessed or given the riches that you have received. Whether with your money, your talents, your time, or your prayers, be generous and remember the poor. The Bible is replete with charges to the Christian to remember the poor.

> All they asked was that we should continue to remember the poor, the very thing I was eager to do. (Galatians 2:10)

> He who oppresses the poor shows contempt for their Maker, but whoever is kind to the needy honors God. (Proverbs 14:31)

> If a man shuts his ears to the cry of the poor, he too will cry out and not be answered. (Proverbs 21:13)

> A generous man will himself be blessed, for he shares his food with the poor. (Proverbs 22:9)

> Do not exploit the poor because they are poor and do not crush the needy in court, for the Lord will take up their case and will plunder those who plunder them. (Proverbs 22:22–23)

> He who gives to the poor will lack nothing, but he who closes his eyes to them receives many curses. (Proverbs 28:27)

> One man gives freely, yet gains even more; another withholds unduly, but comes to poverty. A generous man will prosper; he who refreshes others will himself be refreshed. (Proverbs 11:24–25)

Speak up for those who cannot speak for themselves, for the rights of all who are destitute. Speak up and judge fairly; defend the rights of the poor and needy. (Proverbs 31:8–9)

God has generously blessed us all. Do not hold back in your generosity to those in need. Care for those in need. Bend down in love to lift a brother or a sister in despair. Be wise in the administration of your gifts. Yes, there are those who will prey on your emotions and will take advantage of your generosity. Use wisdom and be prudent. If someone in need has taken unfair advantage of you, learn from the experience and be that more judicious in the future.

CONCLUSION

Well, this is our brief bit of advice. Every subject covered in this work could very easily have volumes written about them and most actually do. We are not blazing new ground or exploring new theories; we are seeking to impart on you those values and virtues we found fundamental and foundational to us during our lives in leading a God-fearing life. Our particular observations are not necessarily the greatest insights the world has known, nor are they unique to us. But they sure were necessary for us in our lives.

These values, lessons, and observations have been around since the beginning of mankind—the same yesterday, today, and forever. They are so simple and yet so easily ignored. What an easy way to have a great life here on earth while at the same time preparing for a blessed life in eternity. So let all of us press on. May we prayerfully ask that you direct your hearts to follow these initiatives.

- Trust the Lord with all our heart, soul, mind, and strength, and heed His commands.
- Love your neighbor as yourself.
- Come to the Lord with a penitent spirit, a broken and contrite heart.
- Actively practice
  o prayer,
  o Bible reading,
  o Sabbath observance,
  o church attendance,
  o tithing, and
  o service to God and His church.
- Love and nurture your family; love your marriage.
- Be patient for all things; be honest.

- Never give up; press on in faith, hope, and love.
- Care for your body, balance your life, and enjoy God's world!

We desire the very best for you and your children. Every parent and grandparent should desire that for his or her grandchildren. In that endeavor, a solid faith in God is the foundation; let no one take that away from you. God chose you for a very special purpose here in life; worship the Lord and hearken unto His calling. Never leave the path. Stay firm in your commitment to pursue the prize of eternal life that is yours to have with our Lord and Savior.

Let us ask one thing of each of you. Pass these lessons on to your children and your grandchildren. Step up and lead in the knowledge and fear of the Lord. Let your children know that your hope and trust is found in the Lord. Go out of your way to help them, nurture them, and support them. Then teach them to pass those same lessons on to their children.

The Lord has never failed His own or deserted His own. He is ever true and faithful, even when we all stray from the path. Always trust Him. His ways are sure. We leave you with our sincere desire for a rich and fulfilling life.

May God give you His rich blessings, and may you abound in mercy and love.